DATE DUE		

CURRENTLY AVAILABLE

BLOOM'S
MAJOR NOVELISTS

Jane Austen
The Brontës
Willa Cather
Stephen Crane
Charles Dickens
Fyodor Dostoevsky
William Faulkner
F. Scott Fitzgerald
Thomas Hardy
Nathaniel Hawthorne
Ernest Hemingway
Henry James
James Joyce
Franz Kafka
D. H. Lawrence
Herman Melville
Toni Morrison
Marcel Proust
John Steinbeck
Stendhal
Leo Tolstoy
Mark Twain
Alice Walker
Edith Wharton
Virginia Woolf

MARCEL PROUST

EDITED AND WITH AN
INTRODUCTION BY HAROLD BLOOM

MARCEL PROUST

EDITED AND WITH AN INTRODUCTION
BY HAROLD BLOOM

A Haights Cross Communications Company

Printed and bound in the United States of America.

First Printing
1 3 5 7 9 8 6 4 2

Library of Congress Cataloging-in-Publication Data
Marcel Proust / edited and with an introduction by Harold Bloom, ed.
p. cm. —(Bloom's major novelists)
Includes bibliographical references and index.
ISBN 0-7910-7029-8
1. Proust, Marcel, 1871–1922—Criticism and interpretation. I.
I. Bloom,
Harold. II. Series.
PQ2631.R63 Z718 2002
843'.912—dc21 2002009997

Chelsea House Publishers
1974 Sproul Road, Suite 400
Broomall, PA 19008-0914

The Chelsea House World Wide Web address is
http://www.chelseahouse.com

Contributing Editor: Michael Cisco

Cover design by Terry Mallon

Layout by EJB Publishing Services

CONTENTS

USER'S GUIDE

This volume is designed to present biographical, critical, and bibliographical information on the author and the author's best-known or most important plays. Following Harold Bloom's editor's note and introduction is a concise biography of the author that discusses major life events and important literary accomplishments. A critical analysis of each play follows, tracing significant themes, patterns, and motifs in the work. An annotated list of characters supplies brief information on the main characters in each play.

A selection of critical extracts, derived from previously published material, follows each thematic analysis. In most cases, these extracts represent the best analysis available from a number of leading critics. Because these extracts are derived from previously published material, they will include the original notations and references when available. Each extract is cited, and readers are encouraged to use the original publications as they continue their research. A bibliography of the author's writings, a list of additional books and articles on the author and their work, and an index of themes and ideas conclude the volume.

As with any study guide, this volume is designed as a supplement to the works being discussed, and is in no way intended as a replacement for those works. The reader is advised to read the text prior to using this study guide, and to keep it accessible for quick reference.

ABOUT THE EDITOR

Harold Bloom is Sterling Professor of the Humanities at Yale University and Henry W. and Albert A. Berg Professor of English at the New York University Graduate School. He is the author of over 20 books, and the editor of more than 30 anthologies of literary criticism.

Professor Bloom's works include *Shelley's Mythmaking* (1959), *The Visionary Company* (1961), *Blake's Apocalypse* (1963), *Yeats* (1970), *A Map of Misreading* (1975), *Kabbalah and Criticism* (1975), *Agon: Toward a Theory of Revisionism* (1982), *The American Religion* (1992), *The Western Canon* (1994), and *Omens of Millennium: The Gnosis of Angels, Dreams, and Resurrection* (1996). *The Anxiety of Influence* (1973) sets forth Professor Bloom's provocative theory of the literary relationships between the great writers and their predecessors. His most recent books include *Shakespeare: The Invention of the Human*, a 1998 National Book Award finalist, *How to Read and Why* (2000), and *Stories and Poems for Extremely Intelligent Children of All Ages* (2001).

Professor Bloom earned his Ph.D. from Yale University in 1955 and has served on the Yale faculty since then. He is a 1985 MacArthur Foundation Award recipient and served as the Charles Eliot Norton Professor of Poetry at Harvard University in 1987–88. In 1999 he was awarded the prestigious American Academy of Arts and Letters Gold Medal for Criticism. Professor Bloom is the editor of several other Chelsea House series in literary criticism, including BLOOM'S MAJOR SHORT STORY WRITERS, BLOOM'S MAJOR NOVELISTS, BLOOM'S MAJOR DRAMATISTS, BLOOM'S MODERN CRITICAL INTERPRETATIONS, BLOOM'S MODERN CRITICAL VIEWS, and BLOOM'S BIOCRITIQUES.

EDITOR'S NOTE

My Introduction meditates upon the relation of Proust's vast book to its vision of privileged moments.

On *In Search of Lost Time* in general, the critic Walter Benjamin ponders Proust's idea of the Image, while the novelist-dramatist Samuel Beckett broods upon Proustian Time.

In regard to the first volume, *Swann's Way*, Wallace Fowlie analyzes Swann's ambivalences, after which Georges Poulét describes Proustian Space, and the stylist Vladimir Nabokov examines prose style in Proust.

Cities of the Plain is adumbrated by Leo Bersani, on the question of jealousy, while Roger Shattuck confronts its major instance, the sexual affair of Marcel and Albertine.

INTRODUCTION
Harold Bloom

Sexual jealousy is the most novelistic of circumstances, just as incest, according to Shelley, is the most poetical of circumstances. Proust is the novelist of our era, even as Freud is our moralist. Both are speculative thinkers, who divide between them the eminence of being the prime wisdom writers of the age.

Proust died in 1922, the year of Freud's grim and splendid essay, "Certain Neurotic Mechanisms in Jealousy, Paranoia, and Homosexuality." Both of them great ironists, tragic celebrants of the comic spirit, Proust and Freud are not much in agreement on jealousy, paranoia, and homosexuality, though both start with the realization that all of us are bisexual in nature.

Freud charmingly begins his essay by remarking that jealousy, like grief, is normal and comes in three stages: *competitive*, or normal, *projected*, *delusional*. The *competitive*, or garden variety, is compounded of grief, due to the loss of the loved object, and of the reactivation of the narcissistic scar, the tragic first loss, by the infant, of the parent of the other sex to the parent of the same sex. As normal, *competitive* jealousy is really normal Hell, Freud genially throws into the compound such delights as enmity against the successful rival, some self-blaming, self-criticism, and a generous portion of bisexuality.

Projected jealousy attributes to the erotic partner one's own actual unfaithfulness or repressed impulses, and is cheerfully regarded by Freud as being relatively innocuous, since its almost delusional character is highly amenable to analytic exposure of unconscious fantasies. But *delusional* jealousy proper is more serious; it also takes its origin in repressed impulses towards infidelity, but the object of those impulses is of one's own sex, and this, for Freud, moves one across the border into paranoia.

What the three stages of jealousy have in common is a bisexual component, since even *projected* jealousy trades in repressed impulses, and these include homosexual desires. Proust, our other authority on jealousy, preferred to call homosexuality "inversion," and in a brilliant mythological fantasia traced the sons of Sodom and the daughters of Gomorrah to the surviving exiles from the Cities of the Plain. Inversion and jealousy, so intimately related in Freud, become in Proust a dialectical pairing, with the aesthetic sensibility linked to both as a third term in a complex series.

On the topos of jealousy, Proust is fecund and generous; no writer has devoted himself so lovingly and brilliantly to expounding and illustrating the emotion, except of course Shakespeare in *Othello* and Hawthorne in *The Scarlet Letter*. Proust's jealous lovers—Swann, Saint-Loup, above all Marcel himself—suffer so intensely that we sometimes need to make an effort not to empathize too closely. It is difficult to determine just what Proust's stance towards their suffering is, partly because Proust's ironies are both pervasive and cunning. Comedy hovers nearby, but even tragicomedy seems an inadequate term for the compulsive sorrows of Proust's protagonists. Swann, after complimenting himself that he has not, by his jealousy, proved to Odette that he loves her too much, falls into the mouth of Hell:

> He never spoke to her of this misadventure, and ceased even to think of it himself. But now and then his thoughts in their wandering course would come upon this memory where it lay unobserved, would startle it into life, thrust it forward into his consciousness, and leave him aching with a sharp, deep-rooted pain. As though it were a bodily pain, Swann's mind was powerless to alleviate it; but at least, in the case of bodily pain, since it is independent of the mind, the mind can dwell upon it, can note that it has diminished, that it has momentarily ceased. But in this case the mind, merely by recalling the pain, created it afresh. To determine not to think of it was to think of it still, to suffer from it still. And when, in conversation with his friends, he forgot about it, suddenly a word casually uttered would make him change countenance like a wounded man when a clumsy hand has touched his aching limb. When he came away from Odette he was happy, he felt calm, he recalled her smiles, of gentle mockery when speaking of this or that other person, of tenderness for himself; he recalled the gravity of her head which she seemed to have lifted from its axis to let it droop and fall, as though in spite of herself, upon his lips, as she had done on the first evening in the carriage, the languishing looks she had given him as she lay in his arms,

> nestling her head against her shoulder as though shrinking from the cold.
>
> But then at once his jealousy, as though it were the shadow of his love, presented him with the complement, with the converse of that new smile with which she had greeted him that very evening—and which now, perversely, mocked Swann and shone with love for another—of that droop of the head, now sinking on to other lips, of all the marks of affection (now given to another) that she had shown to him. And all the voluptuous memories which he bore away from her house were, so to speak, but so many sketches, rough plans like those which a decorator submits to one, enabling Swann to form an idea of the various attitudes, aflame or faint with passion, which she might adopt for others. With the result that he came to regret every pleasure that he tasted in her company, every new caress of which he had been so imprudent as to point out to her the delights, every fresh charm that he found in her, for he knew that, a moment later, they would go to enrich the collection of instruments in his secret torture-chamber.

Jealousy here is a pain experienced by Freud's bodily ego, on the frontier between psyche and body: "To determine not to think of it was to think of it still, to suffer from it still." As the shadow of love, jealousy resembles the shadow cast by the earth up into the heavens, where by tradition it ought to end at the sphere of Venus. Instead, it darkens there, and since the shadow is Freud's reality principle, or our consciousness of our own mortality, Proust's dreadfully persuasive irony is that jealousy exposes not only the arbitrariness of every erotic object-choice but also marks the passage of the loved person into a teleological overdetermination, in which the supposed inevitability of the person is simply a mask for the inevitability of the lover's death. Proust's jealousy thus becomes peculiarly akin to Freud's death drive, since it, too, quests beyond the pleasure/unpleasure principle. Our secret torture-chamber is furnished anew by every recollection of the beloved's erotic prowess, since what delighted us has delighted others.

Swann experiences the terrible conversion of the jealous lover into a parody of the scholar, a conversion to an intellectual pleasure that is more a deviation than an achievement, since no thought can be emancipated from the sexual past of all thought (Freud), if the search for truth is nothing but a search for the sexual past:

> Certainly he suffered as he watched that light, in whose golden atmosphere, behind the closed sash, stirred the unseen and detested pair, as he listened to that murmur which revealed the presence of the man who had crept in after his own departure, the perfidy of Odette, and the pleasures which she was at that moment enjoying with the stranger. And yet he was not sorry he had come; the torment which had forced him to leave his own house had become less acute now that it had become less vague, now that Odette's other life, of which he had had, at that first moment, a sudden helpless suspicion, was definitely there, in the full glare of the lamp-light, almost within his grasp, an unwitting prisoner in that room into which, when he chose, he would force his way to seize it unawares; or rather he would knock on the shutters, as he often did when he came very late, and by that signal Odette would at least learn that he knew, that he had seen the light and had heard the voices, and he himself, who a moment ago had been picturing her as laughing with the other at his illusions, now it was he who saw them, confident in their error, tricked by none other than himself, whom they believed to be far away but who was there, in person, there with a plan, there with the knowledge that he was going, in another minute, to knock on the shutter. And perhaps the almost pleasurable sensation he felt at that moment was something more than the assuagement of a doubt, and of a pain: was an intellectual pleasure. If, since he had fallen in love, things had recovered a little of the delightful interest that they had had for him long ago—though only in so far as they were illuminated by the thought or the memory of Odette—now it was another of the faculties of his studious youth that his jealousy revived, the passion for truth, but for a truth which, too, was interposed between himself and his mistress, receiving its light from her alone, a private and personal truth the sole object of which (an infinitely precious object, and one almost disinterested in its beauty) was Odette's life, her actions, her environment, her plans, her past. At every other period in his life, the little everyday activities of another person had always seemed meaningless to Swann; if gossip

> about such things was repeated to him, he would dismiss it as insignificant, and while he listened it was only the lowest, the most commonplace part of his mind that was engaged; these were the moments when he felt at his most inglorious. But in this strange phase of love the personality of another person becomes so enlarged, so deepened, that the curiosity which he now felt stirring inside him with regard to the smallest details of a woman's daily life, was the same thirst for knowledge with which he had once studied history. And all manner of actions from which hitherto he would have recoiled in shame, such as spying, to-night, outside a window, to-morrow perhaps, for all he knew, putting adroitly provocative questions to casual witnesses, bribing servants, listening at doors, seemed to him now to be precisely on a level with the deciphering of manuscripts, the weighing of evidence, the interpretation of old monuments—so many different methods of scientific investigation with a genuine intellectual value and legitimately employable in the search for truth.

In fact, poor Swann is at the wrong window, and the entire passage is therefore as exquisitely painful as it is comic. What Freud ironically called the overevaluation of the object, the enlargement or deepening of the beloved's personality, begins to work not as one of the enlargements of life (like Proust's own novel) but as the deepening of a personal Hell. Swann plunges downwards and outwards, as he leans "in impotent, blind, dizzy anguish over the bottomless abyss" and reconstructs the petty details of Odette's past life with "as much passion as the aesthete who ransacks the extant documents of fifteenth-century Florence in order to penetrate further into the soul of the Primavera, the fair Vanna or the Venus of Botticelli."

The historicizing aesthete, John Ruskin, say, or Walter Pater, becomes the archetype of the jealous lover, who searches into lost time not for a person, but for an epiphany or moment-of-moments, a privileged fiction of duration:

> When he had been paying social calls Swann would often come home with little time to spare before dinner. At that point in the evening, around six o'clock, when in the old days he used to feel so wretched, he no longer asked himself what Odette might be about, and was hardly at all concerned to hear that she had people with her or had gone out. He recalled at

times that he had once, years ago, tried to read through its envelope a letter addressed by Odette to Forcheville. But this memory was not pleasing to him, and rather than plumb the depths of shame that he felt in it he preferred to indulge in a little grimace, twisting up the corners of his mouth and adding, if need be, a shake of the head which signified "What do I care about it?" True, he considered now that the hypothesis on which he had often dwelt at that time, according to which it was his jealous imagination alone that blackened what was in reality the innocent life of Odette—that this hypothesis (which after all was beneficent, since, so long as his amorous malady had lasted, it had diminished his sufferings by making them seem imaginary) was not the correct one, that it was his jealousy that had seen things in the correct light, and that if Odette had loved him more than he supposed, she had also deceived him more. Formerly, while his sufferings were still keen, he had vowed that, as soon as he had ceased to love Odette and was no longer afraid either of vexing her or of making her believe that he loved her too much, he would give himself the satisfaction of elucidating with her, simply from his love of truth and as a point of historical interest, whether or not Forcheville had been in bed with her that day when he had rung her bell and rapped on her window in vain, and she had written to Forcheville that it was an uncle of hers who had called. But this so interesting problem, which he was only waiting for his jealousy to subside before clearing up, had precisely lost all interest in Swann's eyes when he had ceased to be jealous. Not immediately, however. Long after he had ceased to feel any jealousy with regard to Odette, the memory of that day, that afternoon spent knocking vainly at the little house in the Rue La Pérouse, had continued to torment him. It was as though his jealousy, not dissimilar in that respect from those maladies which appear to have their seat, their centre of contagion, less in certain persons than in certain places, in certain houses, had had for its object not so much Odette herself as that day, that hour in the irrevocable past when Swann had knocked at every entrance to her house in turn, as though that day, that hour alone had caught and preserved a few last fragments of the amorous personality which had once been Swann's, that there alone could he now recapture them. For a long time now it had been a matter of indifference to him whether Odette had been, or was being, unfaithful to him. And yet he had continued for some years to seek out old servants of hers, to such an extent had the painful curiosity persisted in him to know whether on that day, so long ago, at six o'clock, Odette had been in bed with Forcheville. Then that curiosity itself had disappeared, without, however, his abandoning his investigations. He went on trying to discover what no longer interested him, because his old self, though it had shrivelled to extreme decrepitude, still acted mechanically, in accordance with preoccupations so utterly abandoned that Swann could not now succeed even in picturing to himself that anguish—so compelling once that he had been unable to imagine that he would ever be delivered from it, that only the death of the woman he loved (though death, as will be shown later on in this story by a cruel corroboration, in no way diminishes the sufferings caused by jealousy) seemed to him capable of smoothing the path of his life which then seemed impassably obstructed.

Jealousy dies with love, but only with respect to the former beloved. Horribly a life-in-death, jealousy renews itself like the moon, perpetually trying to discover what no longer interests it, even after the object of desire has been literally buried. Its true object is "that day, that hour in the irrevocable past," and even that time was less an actual time than a temporal fiction, an episode in the evanescence of one's own self. Paul de Man's perspective that Proust's deepest insight is the nonexistence of the self founds itself upon this temporal irony of unweaving, this permanent parabasis of meaning. One can remember that even this deconstructive perspective is no more or less privileged than any other Proustian trope, and so cannot give us a truth that Proust himself evades.

II

The bridge between Swann's jealousy and Marcel's is Saint-Loup's jealousy of Rachel, summed up by Proust in one of his magnificently long, baroque paragraphs:

Saint-Loup's letter had come as no surprise to me, even though I had had no news of him since, at the time of my grandmother's illness, he had accused me of perfidy and treachery. I had grasped at once what must have happened. Rachel, who liked to provoke his jealousy (she also had other causes for resentment against me), had persuaded her lover that I had made sly attempts to have relations with her in his absence. It is probable that he continued to believe in the truth of this allegation, but he had ceased to be in love with her, which meant that its truth or falsehood had become a matter of complete indifference to him, and our friendship alone remained. When, on meeting him again, I tried to talk to him about his accusations, he merely gave me a benign and affectionate smile which seemed to be a sort of apology, and then changed the subject. All this was not to say that he did not, a little later, see Rachel occasionally when he was in Paris. Those who have played a big part in one's life very rarely disappear from it suddenly for good. They return to it at odd moments (so much so that people suspect a renewal of old love) before leaving it for ever. Saint-Loup's breach with Rachel had very soon become less painful to him, thanks to the soothing pleasure that was given him by her incessant demands for money. Jealousy, which prolongs the course of love, is not capable of containing many more ingredients than the other products of the imagination. If one takes with one, when one starts on a journey, three or four images which incidentally one is sure to lose on the way (such as the lilies and anemones heaped on the Ponte Vecchio, or the Persian church shrouded in mist), one's trunk is already pretty full. When one leaves a mistress, one would be just as glad, until one had begun to forget her, that she should not become the property of three or four potential protectors whom one pictures in one's mind's eye, of whom, that is to say, one is jealous: all those whom one does not so picture count for nothing. Now frequent demands for money from a cast-off mistress no more give one a complete idea of her life than charts showing a high temperature would of her illness. But the latter would at any rate be an indication that she was ill, and the former furnish a presumption, vague enough it is true, that the forsaken one or forsaker (whichever she be) cannot have found anything very remarkable in the way of rich protectors. And so each demand is welcomed with the joy which a lull produces in the jealous one's sufferings, and answered with the immediate dispatch of money, for naturally

> one does not like to think of her being in want of anything except lovers (one of the three lovers one has in one's mind's eye), until time has enabled one to regain one's composure and to learn one's successor's name without wilting. Sometimes Rachel came in so late at night that she could ask her former lover's permission to lie down beside him until the morning. This was a great comfort to Robert, for it reminded him how intimately, after all, they had lived together, simply to see that even if he took the greater part of the bed for himself it did not in the least interfere with her sleep. He realised that she was more comfortable, lying close to his familiar body, than she would have been elsewhere, that she felt herself by his side—even in an hotel—to be in a bedroom known of old in which one has one's habits, in which one sleeps better. He felt that his shoulders, his limbs, all of him, were for her, even when he was unduly restless from insomnia or thinking of the things he had to do, so entirely usual that they could not disturb her and that the perception of them added still further to her sense of repose.

The heart of this comes in the grandly ironic sentence: "Jealousy, which prolongs the course of love, is not capable of containing many more ingredients than the other products of the imagination." That is hardly a compliment to the capaciousness of the imagination, which scarcely can hold on for long to even three or four images. Saint-Loup, almost on the farthest shore of jealousy, has the obscure comfort of having become, for Rachel, one of those images not quite faded away, when "he felt that his shoulders, his limbs, all of him, were for her," even when he has ceased to be there, or anywhere, for her, or she for him. Outliving love, jealousy has become love's last stand, the final basis for a continuity between two former lovers.

Saint-Loup's bittersweet evanescence as a lover contrasts both with Swann's massive historicism and with the novel's triumphant representation of jealousy, Marcel's monumental search after lost time in the long aftermath of Albertine's death. Another grand link between magnificent jealousies is provided by Swann's observations to Marcel, aesthetic reflections somewhat removed from the pain of earlier realities:

> It occurred to me that Swann must be getting tired of waiting

for me. Moreover I did not wish to be too late in returning home because of Albertine, and, taking leave of Mme de Surgis and M. de Charlus, I went in search of my invalid in the card-room. I asked him whether what he had said to the Prince in their conversation in the garden was really what M. de Bréauté (whom I did not name) had reported to us, about a little play by Bergotte. He burst out laughing: "There's not a word of truth in it, not one, it's a complete fabrication and would have been an utterly stupid thing to say. It's really incredible, this spontaneous generation of falsehood. I won't ask who it was that told you, but it would be really interesting, in a field as limited as this, to work back from one person to another and find out how the story arose. Anyhow, what concern can it be of other people, what the Prince said to me? People are very inquisitive. I've never been inquisitive, except when I was in love, and when I was jealous. And a lot I ever learned! Are you jealous?" I told Swann that I had never experienced jealousy, that I did not even know what it was. "Well, you can count yourself lucky. A little jealousy is not too unpleasant, for two reasons. In the first place, it enables people who are not inquisitive to take an interest in the lives of others, or of one other at any rate. And then it makes one feel the pleasure of possession, of getting into a carriage with a woman, of not allowing her to go about by herself. But that's only in the very first stages of the disease, or when the cure is almost complete. In between, it's the most agonising torment. However, I must confess that I haven't had much experience even of the two pleasures I've mentioned—the first because of my own nature, which is incapable of sustained reflexion; the second because of circumstances, because of the woman, I should say the women, of whom I've been jealous. But that makes no difference. Even when one is no longer attached to things, it's still something to have been attached to them; because it was always for reasons which other people didn't grasp. The memory of those feelings is something that's to be found only in ourselves; we must go back into ourselves to look at it. You mustn't laugh at this idealistic jargon, but what I mean to say is that I've been very fond of life and very fond of art. Well, now that I'm a little too weary to live with other people, those old feelings, so personal and individual, that I had in the past, seem to me—it's the mania of all collectors—very precious. I open my heart to myself like a sort of showcase, and examine one by one all those love affairs of which the rest of the world can have known nothing. And of this collection, to which I'm now even more attached than to my others, I say to myself, rather as Mazarin said of his books, but in fact without the least distress, that it will be very tiresome to have to leave it all. But, to come back to my conversation with the Prince, I shall tell one person only, and that person is going to be you."

We are in the elegy season, ironically balanced between the death of jealousy in Swann and its birth in poor Marcel, who literally does not know that the descent into Avernus beckons. When the vigor of an affirmation has more power than its probability, clearly we are living in a fiction, the metaphor or transference that we call love, and might call jealousy. Into that metaphor, Marcel moves like a sleepwalker, with his obsessions central to *The Captive* and insanely pervasive in *The Fugitive*. A great passage in *The Captive*, which seems a diatribe against jealousy, instead is a passionately ironic celebration of jealousy's aesthetic victory over our merely temporal happiness:

> However, I was still at the first stage of enlightenment with regard to Léa. I was not even aware whether Albertine knew her. No matter, it came to the same thing. I must at all costs prevent her from renewing this acquaintance or making the acquaintance of this stranger at the Trocadéro. I say that I did not know whether she knew Léa or not; yet I must in fact have learned this at Balbec, from Albertine herself. For amnesia obliterated from my mind as well as from Albertine's a great many of the statements that she had made to me. Memory, instead of being a duplicate, always present before one's eyes, of the various events of one's life, is rather a void from which at odd moments a chance resemblance enables one to resuscitate dead recollections; but even then there are innumerable little details which have not fallen into that potential reservoir of memory, and which will remain forever unverifiable. One pays no attention to anything that one does not connect with the real life of the woman one loves; one forgets immediately what she has said to one about such and such an incident or such and such people one does not know, and her expression while she was saying it. And so when, in

> due course, one's jealousy is aroused by these same people, and seeks to ascertain whether or not it is mistaken, whether it is indeed they who are responsible for one's mistress's impatience to go out, and her annoyance when one has prevented her from doing so by returning earlier than usual, one's jealousy, ransacking the past in search of a clue, can find nothing; always retrospective, it is like a historian who has to write the history of a period for which he has no documents; always belated, it dashes like an enraged bull to the spot where it will not find the dazzling, arrogant creature who is tormenting it and whom the crowd admire for his splendour and cunning. Jealousy thrashes around in the void, uncertain as we are in those dreams in which we are distressed because we cannot find in his empty house a person whom we have known well in life, but who here perhaps is another person and has merely borrowed the features of our friend, uncertain as we are even more after we awake when we seek to identify this or that detail of our dream. What was one's mistress's expression when she told one that? Did she not look happy, was she not actually whistling, a thing that she never does unless she has some amorous thought in her mind and finds one's presence importunate and irritating? Did she not tell one something that is contradicted by what she now affirms, that she knows or does not know such and such a person? One does not know, and one will never know; one searches desperately among the unsubstantial fragments of a dream, and all the time one's life with one's mistress goes on, a life that is oblivious of what may well be of importance to one, and attentive to what is perhaps of none, a life hagridden by people who have no real connexion with one, full of lapses of memory, gaps, vain anxieties, a life as illusory as a dream.

Thrashing about in the void of a dream in which a good friend perhaps is another person, jealousy becomes Spenser's Malbecco: "who quite / Forgot he was a man, and jealousy is hight." Yet making life "as illusory as a dream," hagridden by lapses and gaps, is Marcel's accomplishment, and Proust's art. One does not write an other-than-ironic diatribe against one's own art. Proust warily, but with the sureness of a great beast descending upon its helpless prey, approaches the heart of his vision of jealousy, his sense that the emotion is akin to what Freud named as the defense of isolation, in which all context is burned away and a dangerous present replaces all past and all future.

Sexual jealousy in Proust is accompanied by a singular obsessiveness in regard to questions of space and of time. The jealous lover, who, as Proust says, conducts researches comparable to those of the scholar, seeks in his inquiries every detail he can find as to the location and duration of each betrayal and infidelity. Why? Proust has a marvelous passage in *The Fugitive* volume of *Remembrance*:

> It is one of the faculties of jealousy to reveal to us the extent to which the reality of external facts and the sentiments of the heart are an unknown element which lends itself to endless suppositions. We imagine that we know exactly what things are and what people think, for the simple reason that we do not care about them. But as soon as we have a desire to know, as the jealous man has, then it becomes a dizzy kaleidoscope in which we can no longer distinguish anything. Had Albertine been unfaithful to me? With whom? In what house? On what day? On the day when she had said this or that to me, when I remembered that I had in the course of it said this or that? I could not tell. Nor did I know what her feelings were for me, whether they were inspired by self-interest or by affection. And all of a sudden I remembered some trivial incident, for instance that Albertine had wished to go to Saint-Martin-le-Vêtu, saying that the name interested her, and perhaps simply because she had made the acquaintance of some peasant girl who lived there. But it was useless that Aimé should have informed me of what he had learned from the woman at the baths, since Albertine must remain eternally unaware that he had informed me, the need to know having always been exceeded, in my love for Albertine, by the need to show her that I knew; for this broke down the partition of different illusions that stood between us, without having ever had the result of making her love me more, far from it. And now, since she was dead, the second of these needs had been amalgamated with the effect of the first: the need to picture to myself the conversation in which I would have informed her of what I had learned, as vividly as the conversation in which I would have asked her to tell me what I did not know; that is to say, to see her by my side, to hear her answering me kindly, to see her cheeks become plump again, her eyes shed their malice and

> assume an air of melancholy; that is to say, to love her still and to forget the fury of my jealousy in the despair of my loneliness. The painful mystery of this impossibility of ever making known to her what I had learned and of establishing our relations upon the truth of what I had only just discovered (and would not have been able, perhaps, to discover but for her death) substituted its sadness for the more painful mystery of her conduct. What? To have so desperately desired that Albertine—who no longer existed—should know that I had heard the story of the baths! This again was one of the consequences of our inability, when we have to consider the fact of death, to picture to ourselves anything but life. Albertine no longer existed; but to me she was the person who had concealed from me that she had assignations with women at Balbec, who imagined that she had succeeded in keeping me in ignorance of them. When we try to consider what will happen to us after our own death, is it not still our living self which we mistakenly project at that moment? And is it much more absurd, when all is said, to regret that a woman who no longer exists is unaware that we have learned what she was doing six years ago than to desire that of ourselves, who will be dead, the public shall still speak with approval a century hence? If there is more real foundation in the latter than in the former case, the regrets of my retrospective jealousy proceeded none the less from the same optical error as in other men the desire for posthumous fame. And yet, if this impression of the solemn finality of my separation from Albertine had momentarily supplanted my idea of her misdeeds, it only succeeded in aggravating them by bestowing upon them an irremediable character. I saw myself astray in life as on an endless beach where I was alone and where, in whatever direction I might turn, I would never meet her.

"The regrets of my retrospective jealousy proceeded none the less from the same optical error as in other men the desire for posthumous fame"—is that not as much Proust's negative credo as it is Marcel's? Those "other men" include the indubitable precursors, Flaubert and Baudelaire, and Proust himself as well. The aesthetic agon for immortality is an optical error, yet this is one of those errors about life that are necessary for life, as Nietzsche remarked, and is also one of those errors about art that is art. Proust has swerved away from Flaubert into a radical confession of error; the novel is creative envy, love is jealousy, jealousy is the terrible fear that there will not be enough space for oneself (including literary space), and that there never can be enough time for oneself, because death is the reality of one's life. A friend once remarked to me, at the very height of her own jealousy, that jealousy was nothing but a vision of two bodies on a bed, neither of which was one's own, where the hurt resided in the realization that one body ought to have been one's own. Bitter as the remark may have been, it usefully reduces the trope of jealousy to literal fears: where was one's body, where will it be, when will it not be? Our ego is always a bodily ego, Freud insisted, and jealousy joins the bodily ego and the drive as another frontier concept, another vertigo whirling between a desperate inwardness and the injustice of outwardness. Proust, like Freud, goes back after all to the prophet Jeremiah, that uncomfortable sage who proclaimed a new inwardness for his mother's people. The law is written upon our inward parts for Proust also, and the law is justice, but the god of law is a jealous god, though he is certainly not the god of jealousy.

Freud, in "The Passing of the Oedipus Complex," writing two years after Proust's death, set forth a powerful speculation as to the difference between the sexes, a speculation that Proust neither evades nor supports, and yet illuminates, by working out of the world that Freud knows only in the pure good of theory. Freud is properly tentative, but also adroitly forceful:

> Here our material—for some reason we do not understand—becomes far more shadowy and incomplete. The female sex develops an Oedipus-complex, too, a super-ego and a latency period. May one ascribe to it also a phallic organization and a castration complex? The answer is in the affirmative, but it cannot be the same as in the boy. The feministic demand for equal rights between the sexes does not carry far here; the morphological difference must express itself in differences in the development of the mind. "Anatomy is Destiny," to vary a saying of Napoleon's. The little girl's clitoris behaves at first just like a penis, but by comparing herself with a boy playfellow the child perceives that she has "come off short," and takes this fact as ill-treatment and as a reason for feeling inferior. For a time she still consoles herself with the

expectation that later, when she grows up, she will acquire just as big an appendage as a boy. Here the woman's "masculine complex" branches off. The female child does not understand her actual loss as a sex characteristic, but explains it by assuming that at some earlier date she had possessed a member which was just as big and which had later been lost by castration. She does not seem to extend this conclusion about herself to other grown women, but in complete accordance with the phallic phase she ascribes to them large and complete, that is, male, genitalia. The result is an essential difference between her and the boy, namely, that she accepts castration as an established fact, an operation already performed, whereas the boy dreads the possibility of its being performed.

The castration-dread being thus excluded in her case, there falls away a powerful motive towards forming the super-ego and breaking up the infantile genital organization. These changes seem to be due in the girl far more than in the boy to the results of educative influences, of external intimidation threatening the loss of love. The Oedipus-complex in the girl is far simpler, less equivocal, than that of the little possessor of a penis; in my experience it seldom goes beyond the wish to take the mother's place, the feminine attitude towards the father. Acceptance of the loss of a penis is not endured without some attempt at compensation. The girl passes over—by way of a symbolic analogy, one may say—from the penis to a child; her Oedipus-complex culminates in the desire, which is long cherished, to be given a child by her father as a present, to bear him a child. One has the impression that the Oedipus-complex is later gradually abandoned because this wish is never fulfilled. The two desires, to possess a penis and to bear a child, remain powerfully charged with libido in the unconscious and help to prepare the woman's nature for its subsequent sex rôle. The comparative weakness of the sadistic component of the sexual instinct, which may probably be related to the penis-deficiency, facilitates the transformation of directly sexual trends into those inhibited in aim, feelings of tenderness. It must be confessed, however, that on the whole our insight into these processes of development in the girl is unsatisfying, shadowy and incomplete.

Anatomy is destiny in Proust also, but this is anatomy taken up into the mind, as it were. The exiles of Sodom and Gomorrah, more jealous even than other mortals, become monsters of time, yet heroes and heroines of time also. The Oedipus complex never quite passes, in Freud's sense of passing, either in Proust or in his major figures. Freud's castration complex, ultimately the dread of dying, is a metaphor for the same shadowed desire that Proust represents by the complex metaphor of jealousy. The jealous lover fears that he has been castrated, that his place in life has been taken, that true time is over for him. His only recourse is to search for lost time, in the hopeless hope that the aesthetic recovery of illusion and of experience alike, will deceive him in a higher mode than he fears to have been deceived in already.

BIOGRAPHY OF

Marcel Proust

Marcel Proust was born in Auteuil, France, on July 10, 1871; a member of what has come to be known as the "upper middle-class". His father, Dr. Adrien Proust, was a renowned physician and lecturer. His mother, born Jeanne Weil, came from a wealthy Jewish family of considerable status.

From the age of nine, Proust was subject to periodic bouts of anxiety-induced asthma, and other psychosomatic infirmities including indigestion and insomnia. For the rest of his life, Proust would claim chronically bad health. He proved to be a precocious student with a clear aptitude for literary work, and, despite his alleged frailties, performed his single year of mandatory military service happily and successfully. On moving out, in 1890, Proust began his university education, studying law after the urgings of his father, while simultaneously pursuing an extensive program of philosophical reading, and writing brief pieces, mostly society portraits and reviews, for various student journals.

Of all available subjects, high society fascinated Proust the most. While in the army, he had been befriended by Gaston de Caillavet, whose mother presided over one of the most exclusive salons in Paris, and whose lover was the prominent writer, Anatole France. Proust worked feverishly to meet as many important people as possible, and to ingratiate himself to them.

In the mid-1890's, Parisian society was inflamed by controversy over the fate of Alfred Dreyfus, a Jewish captain in the French army, condemned to Devil's Island for passing secret documents to the Germans. Evidence later came to light indicating that Dreyfus had been framed by other officers. The "Dreyfus Affair" polarized French society into "Dreyfusards" and "Anti-Dreyfusards"; along with Anatole France and Emile Zola, Proust was to be found among the Dreyfusards. He attended the trials and participated in the campaign to pressure the government to correct this injustice (Dreyfus was eventually pardoned).

Upon finishing his degrees, Proust half-heartedly took a job as a librarian at the Mazarine Library of the French Institute—a post from which he was routinely absent, and eventually fired, owing to his nocturnal lifestyle, his mania for socializing, and his many affairs with both men and women. In 1901, with the assistance of his new friend, the Comte de Rochefoucauld, Proust finally gained admittance into aristocratic circles, although the most exclusive salons remained closed to him.

In the first decade of the twentieth century, Proust became fascinated with the polymath English critic, John Ruskin. He undertook French translations of two of Ruskin's books, but, despite years of diligent work, his translations were not well-received nor was his interest in Ruskin widely shared. This discouragement was compounded by other, more personal sufferings; the death of his father in 1903, and his mother in 1905. His mother's death, in particular, left Proust nearly incapacitated by grief. Many critics believe that these deaths struck Proust especially hard, because he felt that he had failed to prove himself, to realize the great potential he always had so plainly exhibited, during his parent's lives.

He turned his attention to a long novel, later published posthumously as *Jean Santeuil*, but abandoned it after writing nearly eight hundred pages. Dissatisfied but not discouraged, he tried again, reworking and rethinking the material—the result would eventually be known as *In Search of Lost Time*.

Proust began work on his masterpiece in 1908, under the original title *The Intermittencies of the Heart*, to be further divided into two sections, *Lost Time* and *Time Regained*. By 1912 the first volume, *Swann's Way*, was ready for publication, and the overall project had acquired its famous name. Unfortunately unable to locate a willing publisher, Proust published *Swann's Way* with his own money. The critics received it the following year with disapproval, particularly of Proust's protracted, diaphanous sentences. They were unprepared for his style or for his observations.

In the meantime, Proust's relationship with his secretary and chauffeur, Alfred Agostinelli, whom he had met in 1907, burgeoned, thrived for a time, and then fell apart. Agostinelli left

Proust in 1914; shortly thereafter Proust received the shocking news that Agostinelli, while undergoing pilot training, had been killed when his aircraft crashed into the ocean. This relationship, and its sudden ending, was eventually incorporated into *In Search of Lost Time*, albeit with a female version of Agostinelli.

After his father's death, Proust's finances had been on increasingly shaky ground. In 1914, some ill-advised investments undermined them still further. As the first World War began, the French economy crashed altogether. Despite all this, Proust continued to write feverishly, and the second installment of *In Search of Lost Time*, *Within a Budding Grove*, was accepted by the prestigious Gallimard publishing house. Published after the end of the war, in 1919, *Grove* won for Proust the critical acclaim for which he had thirsted so long. Even those reviewers who had formerly disapproved of his elaborate prose conceded that there was something masterful in his style, and that same year he received the Goncourt Prize for his writing.

With this belated encouragement to bolster his morale, Proust flung himself into his writing, publishing *The Guermantes Way* and *Cities of the Plain* within the next three years. In 1920, he was elected to the French Legion of Honor, in recognition of his contribution to French literature.

In the succeeding two years, Proust's health began to deteriorate rapidly, but throughout this period he devoted all his flagging energies to finishing *In Search of Lost Time*. When a pulmonary infection ended his life on November 18, 1922, the final three volumes were, if unpolished, and as yet unpublished, nevertheless complete. He was interred at Pére-Lachaise, in Paris.

PLOT SUMMARY OF

In Search of Lost Time

[Note—rather than translate the title literally as *In Search of Lost Time*, C. K. Moncrieff, Proust's first English-language translator, chose instead to call the novel *Remembrance of Things Past*, from a line in one of Shakespeare's sonnets. Most contemporary critics prefer the literal title, however, and this title will be employed throughout the following.]

Superficially read, *In Search of Lost Time* is not an eventful book; it is better understood if the reader allows it to alter his or her notion of what an event is. Proust records and describes inner events, most often moments of intellectual or emotional understanding. To the astute and sensitive observer, a dull high-society dinner proves to be as eventful as an historic battle, and as rich a food for thought. The style is symphonic, complex—his sentences string together an extended series of clauses that typically bring the object under discussion into steadily clearer, more detailed focus.

The novel opens with an account of Marcel's difficulties falling asleep, and with dreams (an important theme). Recalling his childhood, Marcel recounts how he was utterly unable to fall asleep without his mother's goodnight kiss. He then describes Combray, his boyhood home, and his visits to his Aunt Leonie there; she would occasionally give him madeleines to eat, having dipped them first in her tea. Years later, Marcel, having forgotten all about it, tastes a madeleine dipped in tea and is astonished to find all of his youth in Combray springing to life again in his mind, as fresh and immediate as if no time had passed. This everyday miracle of involuntary memory will recur throughout the book as the key to the recovery of lost time.

The commonly-excerpted section "Swann in Love" is incorporated into the novel as a capsulized treatment of the themes of love, art, and jealousy which will reappear in Marcel's own adult life later in the novel. Charles Swann, a highly-cultured, sophisticated man, after initially finding her not to be his type, finds himself deeply in love with Odette de Crécy, a superficial high-society butterfly. His love for her, which is mainly an extension of his love for art, and his jealousy, are closely depicted as Swann is drawn to Odette despite her lack of love for him, her infidelity, and her pedestrian mind. The two will eventually marry, although by that time Swann will have ceased to love Odette.

Their daughter, Gilberte, becomes the object of young Marcel's boyish love. In the second volume, *Within a Budding Grove*, Marcel ardently pursues her, with little apparent success, but finds his way into Swann's social circle as a consequence of his attentions. As in the previous volume, Marcel's expectations are subject to constant reversals; mistaking a gesture of enticement made by Gilberte for a dismissal, for example. And what is attractive from a distance is almost never as appealing close up. Long an admirer of the great French writer Bergotte (believed by most critics to be a version of Anatole France), young Marcel is shocked to discover, upon meeting him at Swann's, that Bergotte is nothing like he expected him to be.

Finally, Marcel wills himself to forget Gilberte, convinced that his love for her is not returned. He travels with his grandmother to the coastal town of Balbec, where they meet several members of the aristocratic Guermantes family who will become more prominent in later volumes. Balbec also features a sizeable clique of attractive young girls, with whom Marcel falls in love en masse. One of these young women, Albertine, will later become the sole focus of this love.

The third volume, *The Guermantes Way*, is less personal and more distinctly devoted to a thorough depiction of high society. Having moved with his family into the Hôtel de Guermantes, Marcel is able to observe the Duc and Duchesse de Guermantes, among the most exalted aristocrats in Paris. He longs to enter their world, the world of the fashionable Faubourg Saint-Germain, and eventually his dreams are realized. At a lengthy reception spanning several hundred pages, Proust presents a full spectrum of French aristocrats and their hangers-on, and the gamut of popular opinion on the Dreyfus case. It is at this reception that he formally encounters the Baron de Charlus, a pompous, vainglorious man who takes considerable interest in young Marcel.

After the death of his grandmother, Marcel becomes disillusioned with high society, finding it less glamorous on close inspection than it appeared from a distance. Albertine comes to visit, and Marcel's love affair with her begins. The Baron de Charlus offers his patronage to Marcel, but behaves strangely during Marcel's visit. At the end of the book, Swann explains to the Duc and Duchesse de Guermantes that he is dying of cancer; the Duc and Duchesse receive the news indifferently, searching for the Duchesse's red shoes.

Volume four, *Cities of the Plain*, opens with an explanation of the Baron de Charlus' strange behavior—he, like many other aristocrats, is a homosexual. The first half of this volume is dedicated to a lengthy meditation on the phenomenon of both male and female homosexuality, which will become the enduring theme of the remainder of the work. Two relationships are treated in parallel in *Cities of the Plain*: the love affair between Marcel and Albertine, whom he increasingly (and rightly) suspects of lesbian affairs, and that between the Baron de Charlus and Charles Morel, a gifted but emotionally unstable young violinist. Meanwhile, Marcel's affair with Albertine has varied in intensity on both sides. At the end of the book, having already said he could not possibly marry Albertine, Marcel tells his mother that he *must* marry her.

The marriage does not come about, but Marcel does bring Albertine to live with him in his Parisian apartment in the fifth volume, *The Captive*. Marcel's jealousy quickly becomes the most intense aspect of his feelings for Albertine, and he tries to keep her in the apartment or under a chaperone's observation at all times. In order not to repeat Swann's mistakes, Marcel remains aloof, so that Albertine will not take him for granted. Meanwhile, the Verdurins succeed in their design to break Morel away from Charlus, who is left alone. Marcel decides to end his affair with Albertine, only to discover that she has already left his apartment.

The sixth volume, *The Fugitive*, opens with Marcel's coy attempts to recover Albertine. He writes offhandedly to her, with feigned indifference, hoping to stir up her jealousy and bring her back. Then, in the novel's most painful moment, he receives word that Albertine has been killed in a riding accident. Stunned and reeling, Marcel passes through a period of grieving; then recounts with unflinching honesty his growing indifference to her loss. Gilberte, now grown, has married Marcel's good friend Saint-Loup, who turns out himself to be more interested in men than women. Marcel allows Gilberte to distract him from his grief, and their romance briefly and faintly revives.

The pace of the novel accelerates at the opening of the seventh and final volume, *The Past Recaptured*. The war has broken out; Saint-Loup is killed at the front. Charlus has fallen into disrepute for his belligerently pro-German stance. The key incident in this final installment takes place at a reception given by Mme de Verdurin, celebrating her marriage to the Prince de Guermantes. Marcel, who alludes to his ill health, attends the reception and encounters most of the characters still living; Odette is characteristically unchanged, but the rest are all marked by the amount of time that has passed. On his way in, he bumps into a garrulous, decrepit old man in the street, who turns out to be Charlus; now badly deteriorated, Charlus has not been invited to the reception. Tripping over uneven paving stones as he goes inside, Marcel experiences a flash of involuntary memory; another such flash occurs shortly thereafter, and these experiences cause him to reflect on the uncanny operation of memory. These brief visitations bring him not the dead, photographic remains of the past, but the living presence of the past. He has long tried to achieve something as a writer, but to no success; not only has he failed to win any glory as a writer, but he has yet to experience true inspiration. These moments of involuntary memory supply him with that longed-for inspiration, and he realizes his literary mission is to recapture his past in living form, not as a historical record but in its vibrant presence. Any true depiction of a person's life must take into account not so much the external and superficial facts of time and place, but the rich inner events so poorly understood at the time, the complex and dimly-visible heap of artistic associations, dreams, and memories that always accompany present experience.

At the end of *In Search of Lost Time*, Marcel, haunted by the possibility of his own immanent death due to ill-health, expresses his hope that he will have time enough to realize his great literary project, which will be nothing less than *In Search of Lost Time* itself, making the novel the story of its own preconditions for existing. In closing, Marcel points out that, while individual persons are almost ludicrously small in space, we are all monumentally vast in the dimension of time.

LIST OF CHARACTERS IN
In Search of Lost Time

"Marcel" the anonymous narrator, is a middle-aged man looking back on his childhood. Sensitive, intelligent, literary, if somewhat effete, and above all looking to find and fulfill his vocation in life.

Marcel's mother finds her son somewhat too clinging and dependent, but who is one of the few prominent characters in the novel without significant flaws. She will come to resemble Marcel's grandmother more and more.

Marcel's father is a distant figure who plays little role in Marcel's life. He has great power to affect his son, but applies it inconsistently and distractedly.

Marcel's grandmother is perhaps the only figure in *In Search of Lost Time* who is not depicted as ultimately selfish. She has her "principles," which include regular walks in the garden, even in the rain, and keeping her husband from drinking brandy at any cost. The realization of her death causes Marcel to experience a minor epiphany.

Marcel's grandfather is a knowing old man who takes great pleasure in mischieviously disobeying and upsetting his wife.

Françoise is the family servant who will attend Marcel throughout the novel. She is a hard woman, capable of great sympathy for the sufferings of those in far-away places and oblivious to the suffering of those around her.

Odette de Crécy, later Odette Swann, and then Odette Forcheville is a promiscuous, bisexual high-society courtesan, affecting a certain poise and sophistication, but a basically selfish, shallow, unintelligent woman.

Charles Swann is an exemplar of elegant taste and exquisite manners, aesthetic judgement and lofty, but unostentatious, intellect. He will fall incongruously in love with Odette de Crécy, and eventually marry her. For most of the novel, he is quietly dying of cancer.

Gilberte Swann is the daughter of Charles and Odette Swann. Encountered again as an adult, she has become a snobbish social climber. Eventually marries Robert de Saint-Loup.

Aunt Léonie is Marcel's invalid aunt in Combray, out of whose cup of tea the entire boyhood section grows. A kind, pious woman, who represents bourgeois respectability.

Madame Verdurin maintains a middlebrow bourgeois salon, which serves to bring Odette and Swann together. Lacking status, she makes up for it with an affected aesthetic snobbery. After her husband's death, she will marry the Prince de Guermantes and enter the aristocracy.

Monsieur Verdurin is Mme Verdurin's overbearing, slightly ogrish husband, who is likewise more concerned with his social standing than with the high art and culture he pretends to understand.

Bergotte is young Marcel's literary idol. While he does not turn out to be the elegant figure Marcel imagined him to be, Bergotte, though somewhat rough of manner, is an unusually perceptive and intelligent man.

Elstir is a painter modelled on Manet. Living in Balbec, he has painted both the young ladies whom young Marcel finds so appealing and Odette de Crécy in an earlier life. A friend of Albertine's.

Doctor Cottard is the comically vapid hanger-on with the Verdurins. A quack who mistakenly believes himself to be the soul of wit, constantly interjecting into other people's conversations with corny puns and lame quotations.

Bloch is the hyper-sensitive young Jewish student constantly making social gaffes. He speaks in an overly-elaborate, literary manner that is clearly meant to cover his insecurities about being accepted. Possibly a caricature of Proust himself.

Forcheville, Odette's haughty lover, is from the Verdurin circle. A pompous, insulting man.

the Baron de Charlus, whose vanity and arrogance are counterbalanced by the pain and shame associated with his homosexuality, and the abuse he receives from the cold-hearted Morel.

the Duc de Guermantes, wealthy, philandering, and aloof; an almost completely selfish man.

the Duchesse de Guermantes, an object of fascination, and brief infatuation, for Marcel as a boy and young man; beautiful, witty, with a vicious sense of humor and a great talent for mimicry.

Charles Morel, the mercurial, ill-tempered violinist and object of the Baron de Charlus' affections. He is cold, calculating, and utterly selfish, unfaithful to the Baron and grasping after his money.

Prince de Guermantes exudes an aura of lofty authority and inaccessibility. Like many other characters, he is secretly conducting homosexual affairs, even with Morel. Upon his wife's death, he will marry the widowed Mme Verdurin.

Princesse de Guermantes, stands at the apex of Parisian society, a woman of celebrated beauty and exquisite taste. She harbors a completely hopeless love for Charlus.

Albertine is a beautiful, dark-haired girl, who conceals a strong attraction to other girls. She is the love of Marcel's life, a witty, intelligent, increasingly well-cultivated young woman, addicted to white lies and clandestine meetings. After her unexpected death, Marcel will uncover the extensive history of her lesbian affairs.

Andrée is another of the pretty young girls of Balbec, Albertine's wry friend, with whom she occasionally dallies. Marcel routinely feigns interest in her, to make Albertine jealous.

Jupien is a former tailor with a shop in the Hôtel de Guermantes, and Charlus' sometime lover. He facilitates Charlus' relationship with Morel, and puts forward Morel's plan to marry his niece.

Robert de Saint-Loup is a Guermantes and one of Marcel's boyhood friends from Balbec. An affable young man who conceals his interest in men behind a slightly over-emphatic gallantry to women. He will marry Gilberte Swann.

Norpois, a diplomat and intellectual, lover of Mme de Villeparisis and friend of Marcel's family. Copious advice and insight issue from him through the course of the novel, and he advises Marcel's father to encourage him to write.

Marquise de Villeparisis is an unostentatious older woman who gives Marcel his first access to the Guermantes circle. She represents a bygone era of the French aristocracy.

CRITICAL VIEWS OF
In Search of Lost Time

WALTER BENJAMIN ON PROUST'S CONCEPT OF THE IMAGE

[Author of "The Work of Art in the Age of Mechanical Reproduction," Walter Benjamin's writings, particularly those compiled and translated in *Illuminations*, have been consistently popular among students of literature from the 1950s to the present. This is an excerpt from his essay, "The Image of Proust."]

The thirteen volumes of Marcel Proust's *À la Recherche du temps perdu* are the result of an unconstruable synthesis in which the absorption of a mystic, the art of a prose writer, the verve of a satirist, the erudition of a scholar, and the self-consciousness of a monomaniac have combined in an autobiographical work. It has rightly been said that all great works of literature found a genre or dissolve one—that they are, in other words, special cases. Among these cases this is one of the most unfathomable. From its structure, which is fiction, autobiography, and commentary in one, to the syntax of endless sentences (the Nile of language, which here overflows and fructifies the regions of truth), everything transcends the norm. The first revealing observation that strikes one is that this great special case of literature at the same time constitutes its greatest achievement of recent decades. The conditions under which it was created were extremely unhealthy: an unusual malady, extraordinary wealth, and an abnormal disposition. This is not a model life in every respect, but everything about it is exemplary. The outstanding literary achievement of our time is assigned a place in the heart of the impossible, at the center—and also at the point of indifference—of all dangers, and it marks this great realization of a "lifework" as the last for a long time. The image of Proust is the highest physiognomic expression which the irresistibly growing discrepancy between literature and life was able to assume. This is the lesson which justifies the attempt to evoke this image.

We know that in his work Proust did not describe a life as it actually was, but a life as it was remembered by the one who had lived it. And yet even this statement is imprecise and far too crude. For the important thing for the remembering author is not what he experienced, but the weaving of his memory, the Penelope work of recollection. Or should one call it, rather, a Penelope work of forgetting? Is not the involuntary recollection, Proust's *mémoire involontaire*, much closer to forgetting than what is usually called memory? And is not this work of spontaneous recollection, in which remembrance is the woof and forgetting the warf, a counterpart to Penelope's work rather than its likeness? For here the day unravels what the night has woven. When we awake each morning, we hold in our hands, usually weakly and loosely, but a few fringes of the tapestry of lived life, as loomed for us by forgetting. However, with our purposeful activity and, even more, our purposive remembering each day unravels the web and the ornaments of forgetting. This is why Proust finally turned his days into nights, devoting all his hours to undisturbed work in his darkened room with artificial illumination, so that none of those intricate arabesques might escape him.

The Latin word *textum* means "web." No one's text is more tightly woven than Marcel Proust's; to him nothing was tight or durable enough. From his publisher Gallimard we know that Proust's proofreading habits were the despair of the typesetters. The galleys always went back covered with marginal notes, but not a single misprint had been corrected; all available space had been used for fresh text. Thus the laws of remembrance were operative even within the confines of the work. For an experienced event is finite—at any rate, confined to one sphere of experience; a remembered event is infinite, because it is only a key to everything that happened before it and after it. There is yet another sense in which memory issues strict weaving regulations. Only the *actus purus* of recollection itself not the author or the plot, constitutes the unity of the text. One may even say that the intermittence of author and plot is only the reverse of the continuum of memory, the pattern on the back side of the tapestry. This is what Proust meant, and this is how he must be understood, when he said that he would prefer to see his entire work printed in one volume in two columns and without any paragraphs.

What was it that Proust sought so frenetically? What was at the bottom of these infinite efforts? Can we say that all lives, works, and deeds that matter were never anything but the undisturbed unfolding of the most banal, most fleeting, most sentimental, weakest hour in the life of the one to whom they pertain? When Proust in a well-known passage described the hour that was most his own, he did it in such a way that everyone can find it in his own existence. We might almost call it an everyday hour; it comes with the night, a lost twittering of birds, or a breath drawn at the sill of in open window. And there is no telling what encounters would be in store for us if we were less inclined to give in to sleep. Proust did not give in to sleep. And yet—or, rather, precisely for this reason—Jean Cocteau was able to say in a beautiful essay that the intonation of Proust's voice obeyed the laws of night and honey. By submitting to these laws he conquered the hopeless sadness within him (what he once called "*l'imperfection incurable dans l'essence même du présent*"*), and from the honeycombs of memory he built a house for the swarm of his thoughts. Cocteau recognized what really should have been the major concern of all readers of Proust and yet has served no one as the pivotal point of his reflections or his affection. He recognized Proust's blind, senseless, frenzied quest for happiness. It shone from his eyes; they were not happy, but in them there lay fortune as it lies in gambling or in love. Nor is it hard to say why this paralyzing, explosive will to happiness which pervades Proust's writings is so seldom comprehended by his readers. In many places Proust himself made it easy for them to view this *oeuvre*, too, from the time-tested, comfortable perspective of resignation, heroism, asceticism. After all, nothing makes more sense to the model pupils of life than the notion that a great achievement is the fruit of toil, misery, and disappointment. The idea that happiness could have a share in beauty would be too much of a good thing, something that their *ressentiment* would never get over.

There is a dual will to happiness, a dialectics of happiness: a hymnic and an elegiac form. The one is the unheard-of, the unprecedented, the height; the other, the eternal repetition, the eternal restoration of the original, the first happiness. It is this elegiac idea of happiness—it could also be called Eleatic—which for Proust transforms existence into a preserve of memory. To it he sacrificed in his life friends and companionship, in his works plot, unity of characters, the flow of the narration, the play of the imagination. Max Unold, one of Proust's more discerning readers, fastened on the "boredom" thus created in Proust's writings and likened it to "pointless stories." "Proust managed to make the pointless story interesting. He says: 'Imagine, dear reader, yesterday I was dunking a cookie in my tea when it occurred to me that as a child I spent some time in the country.' For this he uses eighty pages, and it is so fascinating that you think you are no longer the listener but the daydreamer himself." In such stories—"all ordinary dreams turn into pointless stories as soon as one tells them to someone"—Unold has discovered the bridge to the dream. No synthetic interpretation of Proust can disregard it. Enough inconspicuous gates lead into it—Proust's frenetically studying resemblances, his impassioned cult of similarity. The true signs of its hegemony do not become obvious where he suddenly and startlingly uncovers similarities in actions, physiognomies, or speech mannerisms. The similarity of one thing to another which we are used to, which occupies us in a wakeful state, reflect only vaguely the deeper resemblance of the dream world in which everything that happens appears not in identical but in similar guise, opaquely similar one to another. Children know a symbol of this world: the stocking which has the structure of this dream world when, rolled up in the laundry hamper, it is a "bag" and a "present" at the same time. And just as children do not tire of quickly changing the bag and its contents into a third thing—namely, a stocking—Proust could not get his fill of emptying the dummy, his self, at one stroke in order to keep garnering that third thing, the image which satisfied his curiosity—indeed, assuaged his homesickness. He lay on his bed racked with homesickness, homesick for the world distorted in the state of resemblance, a world in which the true surrealist face of existence breaks through. To this world belongs what happens in Proust, and the deliberate and fastidious way in which it appears. It is never isolated, rhetorical, or visionary; carefully heralded and securely supported, it bears a fragile, precious reality; the image. It detaches itself from the structure of Proust's sentences as that summer day at Balbec—old, immemorial, mummified—emerged from the lace curtains under Françoise's hands.

NOTE

* "... the incurable imperfection in the very essence of the present moment."

—Walter Benjamin, *Illuminations*, (New York: Schocken Books, 1968 – article first published in *Literarische Welt*, 1929): 201–205.

SAMUEL BECKETT ON PROUST'S TREATMENT OF CHARACTER AND TIME

[Samuel Beckett was one of the most celebrated literary figures of the twentieth century, author of numerous plays including "Waiting for Godot" and "Endgame", and novels such as *Molloy*, *Malone Dies*, and *The Unnameable*. Beckett was awarded the Nobel Prize in 1969. In this extract from his first published work, he characterizes Proust's literary sense of the relationship of character and time.]

Proust's creatures, then, are victims of this predominating condition and circumstance—Time; victims as lower organisms, conscious only of two dimensions and suddenly confronted with the mystery of height, are victims: victims and prisoners. There is no escape from the hours and the days. Neither from tomorrow nor from yesterday. There is no escape from yesterday because yesterday has deformed us, or been deformed by us. The mood is of no importance. Deformation has taken place. Yesterday is not a milestone that has been passed, but a daystone on the beaten track of the years, and irremediably part of us, within us, heavy and dangerous. We are not merely more weary because of yesterday, we are other, no longer what we were before the calamity of yesterday. A calamitous day, but calamitous not necessarily in content. The good or evil disposition of the object has neither reality nor significance. The immediate joys and sorrows of the body and the intelligence are so many superfoetations. Such as it was, it has been assimilated to the only world that has reality and significance, the world of our own latent consciousness, and its cosmography has suffered a dislocation. So that we are rather in the position of Tantalus, with this difference, that we allow ourselves to be tantalised. And possibly the perpetuum mobile of our disillusions is subject to more variety. The aspirations of yesterday were valid for yesterday's ego, not for to-day's. We are disappointed at the nullity of what we are pleased to call attainment. But what is attainment? The identification of the subject with the object of his desire. The subject has died—and perhaps many times—on the way. For subject B to be disappointed by the banality of an object chosen by subject A is as illogical as to expect one's hunger to be dissipated by the spectacle of Uncle eating his dinner. Even suppose that by one of those rare miracles of coincidence, when the calendar of facts runs parallel to the calendar of feelings, realisation takes place, that the object of desire (in the strictest sense of that malady) is achieved by the subject, then the congruence is so perfect, the time-state of attainment eliminates so accurately the time-state of aspiration, that the actual seems the inevitable, and, all conscious intellectual effort to reconstitute the invisible and unthinkable as a reality being fruitless, we are incapable of appreciating our joy by comparing it with our sorrow. Voluntary memory (Proust repeats it ad nauseam) is of no value as an instrument of evocation, and provides an image as far removed from the real as the myth of our imagination or the caricature furnished by direct perception. There is only one real impression and one adequate mode of evocation. Over neither have we the least control. That reality and that mode will be discussed in their proper place.

But the poisonous ingenuity of Time in the science of affliction is not limited to its action on the subject, that action, as has been shown, resulting in an unceasing modification of his personality, whose permanent reality, if any, can only be apprehended as a retrospective hypothesis. The individual is the seat of a constant process of decantation, decantation from the vessel containing the fluid of future time, sluggish, pale and monochrome, to the vessel containing the fluid of past time, agitated and multicoloured by the phenomena of its hours. Generally speaking, the former is innocuous, amorphous, without character, without any Borgian virtue. Lazily considered in anticipation and in the haze of our smug will to live, of our pernicious and incurable optimism, it seems exempt from the bitterness of fatality: in store for us, not in store in us. On occasions, however, it is capable of supplementing the labours of its colleague. It is only necessary for its surface to be broken by a date, by any temporal specification allowing us to measure the days that separate us from a menace—or a promise. Swann, for example, contemplates with doleful resignation the months that he must spend away from Odette during the summer. One day Odette says: 'Forcheville (her lover, and, after the death of Swann, her husband) is going to Egypt at Pentecost.' Swann translates: 'I am going with Forcheville to Egypt at Pentecost.' The fluid of future time freezes, and poor Swann, face to face with the *future* reality of Odette and Forcheville in Egypt, suffers more grievously than even at the misery of his present condition. The narrator's desire to see La Berma in *Phèdre* is stimulated more violently by the announcement 'Doors closed at two o'clock' than by the mystery of Bergotte's 'Jansenist pallor and solar myth.' His indifference at parting from Albertine at the end of the day in Balbec is transformed into the most horrible anxiety by a simple remark addressed by her to her aunt or to a friend: 'To-morrow, then, at half-past eight.' The tacit understanding that the future can be controlled is destroyed. The future event cannot be focussed, its implications cannot be seized, until it is definitely situated and a date assigned to it. When Albertine was his prisoner, the possibility of her escape did not seriously disturb him, because it was indistinct and abstract, like the possibility of death. Whatever opinion we may be pleased to hold on the subject of death, we may be sure that it is meaningless and valueless. Death has not required us to keep a day free. The art of publicity has been revolutionised by a similar consideration. Thus I am exhorted, not merely to try the aperient of the Shepherd, but to try it at seven o'clock.

So far we have considered a mobile subject before an ideal object, immutable and incorruptible. But our vulgar perception is not concerned with other than vulgar phenomena. Exemption from intrinsic flux in a given object does not change the fact that it is the correlative of a subject that does not enjoy such immunity. The observer infects the observed with his own mobility. Moreover, when it is a case of human intercourse, we are faced by the problem of an object whose mobility is not merely a function of the subject's, but independent and personal: two separate and immanent dynamisms related by no system of synchronisation. So that whatever the object, our thirst for possession is, by definition, insatiable. At the best, all that is realised in Time (all Time produce), whether in Art or Life, can only be possessed successively, by a series of partial annexations—and never integrally and at once. The tragedy of the Marcel-Albertine liaison is the type-tragedy of the human relationship whose failure is preordained. My analysis of that central catastrophe will clarify this too abstract and arbitrary statement of Proust's pessimism. But for every tumour a scalpel and a compress. Memory and Habit are attributes of the Time cancer. They control the most simple Proustian episode, and an understanding of their mechanism must precede any particular analysis of their application. They are the flying buttresses of the temple raised to commemorate the wisdom of the architect that is also the wisdom of all the sages, from Brahma to Leopardi, the wisdom that consists not in the satisfaction but in the ablation of desire:

> 'In noi di cari inganni
> non che la speme, il desiderio è spento.'

—Samuel Beckett, *Proust*, (New York: Grove Press, 1931): pp 2–7.

Germaine Brée on the Proustian "Romance"

[Former president of the Modern Language Association and chair of the French department at New York University, Germaine Brée is the author of *Gide*, *Camus*, and *Camus and Sartre*. This is her characterization of the role of romantic love in the novel.]

Love is an important theme in *A la Recherche du Temps perdu*, both by virtue of the space devoted to the successive loves of Swann and the narrator, of Saint-Loup and Charlus, and because of the rôle it plays in the reflections and behavior of Proust's characters. The narrator's constant preoccupation with his desire and hope for love is the most influential factor in all his dreams as a child, adolescent, and young man. He dwells upon the image of almost every woman he knows, provided that she is at once nearby and faraway, visible yet unknown. Gilberte Swann, Mademoiselle de Stermaria, the flock of young girls at Balbec, Madame de Guermantes, a peasant girl glimpsed on the road—he desires them all. This longing for love is at first nebulous, associated in his mind with the novels and poetry he reads, and is imbued with a timeless and mysterious quality. He always associates the word "love" with the idea of "vague and superhuman" bliss. For a long time it remains a dream for him, even when he focusses his attention upon Gilberte who is real. Nevertheless, the narrator's existence is oriented by his phantasy of love; if judged without reference to its influence, some of his actions would remain completely incomprehensible—his rovings in the Champs Elysées, his haunting of the streets in Swann's neighborhood and of the Guermantes' town house, his walks along the promenade in Balbec are just as strange as Charlus' behaviour if they are considered apart from the obsession with the possibility of love which motivates them. In one sense it can be said that the most consistent motivating force in the narrator's rather easy-going life is his desire to realize the dream of happiness promised by the word "love." For a long time he is "in search" of something he thinks love will give him.

In the first part of the novel, *Un Amour de Swann*, the harmonious development of this theme, although it perfectly counterbalances the chapter on Combray, can be considered as a separate story. Like *Tristan et Iseult*, *La Princesse de Clèves*, or *Adolphe*, it can be read as a sort of monograph, a "tale," developed in a single movement, stylized and pure. It could take its place among the great French love stories which go back to the Middle Ages and in this connotation would present, through Swann, a new psychological view of love: the story, complete in itself, of the variations of this particular kind of love as an isolated phenomenon. It would, however, be contrary to the spirit in which *A la Recherche du Temps perdu* is conceived that Proust should have inserted into the novel an episode separable from the whole. *Un Amour de Swann* is placed between the end of Combray and the prelude to the *Jeunes filles en fleurs*. Swann plays an important rôle in all three parts; his prestige in the child's eyes adumbrates his entrance on the stage, while at the same time his story gives the narrator's tale a dimension in time, opening up a perspective on a past which reaches further back than the narrator's. In addition, Swann's story serves as a background for the narrator's dreams of love and for his first experiment in love with Gilberte, and it enriches them. The narrator dreams of a sentimental, idealized, rather tame love which is markedly different from the emotions experienced by Swann. This divergence is one of the essential elements in Proust's orchestration of the theme; it is to be found in all his accounts of various liaisons.

The narrator's preconceived notions of love, which are centered in a set of images, are never borne out by reality; in his association with Gilberte, these images are never realized but he finds himself flooded by emotions through which Gilberte becomes his personification of love. The world in which Swann's love takes place lies between these two, and the realization of that love, both pathetic and trivial, already foreshadows the ambiguity of the word "love" and the inevitable failure of the search for happiness through love. This search is basically the quest for something else which Swann is never able to discern. The enigma propounded to him by Vinteuil's musical phrase in relation to his love for Odette remains unsolved, but the relationship between love, happiness, suffering, and art is established. We are at the very heart of the relationships which give meaning not only to the narrator's experience, but to the structure of *A la Recherche du Temps perdu* itself. It is only through the experience of characters other than the child that Proust is able to present the love theme with all its overtones at the very beginning of his novel. The child experiences love in the form of images: the image of the "lady in pink," or of Montjouvain, so distressingly different from the dream inspired by his reading. It is Swann's experience that gives depth to these images. All the other attempts at love, either episodic or carefully developed, are merely variations of Swann's love.

Each of these "romances" is, like Swann's, circumscribed by time. Each begins, develops, and ends. For a certain length of time romance absorbs the whole existence of the characters, and even transforms them, but they later resume the normal rhythm of an existence scarcely marked by the experience except for minor outward manifestations, habits acquired while the "romance" lasted. The deterioration of Swann's social life after his marriage with Odette, or Saint-Loup's calculated mannerisms, for example, are the traces left by a love which has run its course. Every love story leaves in its wake only a few images, some material facts, and the knowledge that it once was real. The actual experience of love is obliterated little by little until it is almost entirely forgotten.

All these Proustian "romances" follow each other closely and are all eventually lost in the passage of time. When we first catch a glimpse of Swann, the elegant, cultivated, amiable man of the world who holds himself aloof from any profound emotion, his love is far behind him and has long ago lost any significance for him. If he thinks about it at all, it is with a faint feeling of surprise at having "lost" in this way so many years of his life. No matter how painful and all-absorbing a love affair may temporarily appear to those who experience it, it is never in *A la Recherche du Temps perdu* more than an episode, and derives its significance precisely from that fact. This is never the case in the classical love story, although Proust seems deliberately to use the terminology of that kind of story when he describes the emotions of his characters. And they also allude to the "romance"[1] they are living. All of them, with the possible exception of Swann, want more or less consciously to play their part in a great romantic novel. And that is in fact what they do, but not as they imagine it, not according to the tenets of the classical tale in which love per se, happy or unhappy, has intrinsic significance for the individual.

Among these love stories, those of Charlus and Saint-Loup are described objectively. Swann's is presented as it was actually lived by him, but the narrator evokes it from the past just as he evokes his own loves from a past more or less remote, in order to evaluate and analyze them. He merely regards his own loves with a greater degree of subjectivity. The story of Saint-Loup's love for Rachel, and of Charlus' love for Morel are episodes within the novel as a whole, and appear and disappear according to Saint-Loup's and Charlus' position in the narrator's field of vision. On the other hand, Swann's and the narrator's loves have their clearly allotted place in the novel. Swann and Odette, Gilberte and the narrator, Albertine and the narrator, are at first mingled with a great number of other characters though they are somewhat more carefully delineated; then, rather slowly, each couple is detached from the group and moves into the foreground as the other characters recede. The couple play their love scene, supplemented by a few minor figures. The converse movement then takes place, and each of the two partners resumes his autonomy, but not simultaneously. The image of the woman disappears first, leaving the man who loves her, alone, in the foreground of the story; then he too "returns" to his social milieu as Swann returns to the Saint-Euvertes or the narrator to Mme Swann's salon.

Un Amour de Swann, the whole beginning of the *Jeunes filles en fleurs*, *La Prisonnière*, and *Albertine disparue* thus create, within the very heart of the complex and crowded Proustian world in which the whole human comedy is played, smaller more stable worlds which attempt, without ever succeeding, to achieve autonomy by eliminating everything that has no direct bearing upon them. By this very fact they are doomed to eventual failure, since they are constructed on the most shifting soil imaginable, that of the Proustian personality. To love Odette, Gilberte, and Albertine is to assert a belief in the physical existence of a human individuality which coincides with a particular human body. And even human bodies, which seem to guarantee that individuals exist are portrayed by Proust as frighteningly ubiquitous in time and space; their variations reveal only in part those which the individuals who possess them can undergo.

NOTE

1. For example: vol. I, p. 628; "It is with her that I shall have my romance." Vol. III, pp. 654, 679: "The sterile romance" which the narrator builds up about Madame de Guermantes.

—Germaine Brée, *Marcel Proust and Deliverance from Time*, (New Brunswick, N.J.: Rutgers University Press, 1956): 131–135.

WILLIAM STEWART BELL ON DREAMS AND IDENTITY

[Here he describes how dreams offer characters in the novel an opportunity to re-experience past selves.]

Dreams and Memory: Discovery of the Unity of the Self

The dreams that occur throughout *La Recherche* are not recapitulations of the events of the dreamer's past life; though they are based upon it, they are a re-creation of this life, involving a re-becoming of the person as he was in the past. Swann's desire to recover the Odette of the past did not arise from any great change in Odette herself, but rather from Swann's own emotional change over a period of time. He therefore, had to recapture the Swann of the time of their first meeting. Marcel, as the most prolific dreamer in the novel, underwent such experiences often.[15]

Dreams, such as Swann's, were used to reveal laws about the type of memory that was Proust's special concern: "Now our love memories present no exception to the general rules of memory, which in turn are governed by the still more general rules of habit" (I, 488 [I, 643]). The love memories were revived in dreams, just as they were by the chance encounter with a phrase such as "the Secretary to the Ministry of Posts and his family," which recalled Gilberte. The conscious memory, vitiated by habit, was ineffective in re-creating the past; unconscious phenomena alone were capable of true memory. Proust offers a striking example with regard to the revival of the memory of Albertine after her death:

> We exist only by virtue of what we possess, we possess only what is really present to us, and so many of our memories, our humours, our ideas set out to voyage far away from us, until they are lost to sight! Then we can no longer make them enter into our reckoning of the total which is our personality. But they know of secret paths by which to return to us. And on certain nights ... I found a whole fleet of memories which had come to cruise upon the surface of my clearest consciousness, and seemed marvelously distinct. [II, 725 (III, 488)]

One of Proust's major concerns was with "the total which is our personality." At first glance, the dream appears to oppose this idea of unity. One of the salient lessons of the two sequences of dreams illustrating the intermissions is the multiplicity of the self—"innumerable and humble 'selves'" (II, 683 [III, 430]) which had to be notified that Albertine was gone. In this same passage Proust refers to a dream found in the opening pages of *Swann* as an example of the existence of other "selves": "There were some of these 'selves' which I had not encountered for a long time past. For instance ... the 'self' that I was when I was having my hair cut. I had forgotten this 'self' ..." (II, 683–84 [III, 430–31]).

The discontinuity created by this succession of differing selves tends to give the reader a feeling of malaise. Pierre-Henri Simon finds in Proust's work a succession of vertiginous and painful passages in which the self is portrayed as shattered into tiny pieces, divided into incommunicable states, completely isolated from each other.[16] It would seem that Marcel felt this discomfort keenly and that, when he tried to reconstruct the past, he found only a series of dead selves juxtaposed. This search for continuity was a frequent concern to other writers of the nineteenth and early twentieth centuries[17] who, in their attempts to escape from themselves in order to attain the absolute, found that their efforts to abolish the self gave rise to a new anguish: the self came to doubt its own coherence, to find only a series of separate moments lacking in unity and a personality that was broken up and diffused.

Proust pondered this apparent lack of unity and observed carefully the process of awakening in an effort to learn how, after having revived a former self, the current personality is recovered:

> Then from those profound slumbers we awake in a dawn, not knowing who we are, being nobody, newly born, ready for anything, our brain being emptied of that past which was previously our life.... Then, from the black tempest through which we seem to have passed (but we do not even say *we*), we emerge prostrate, without a thought, a *we* that is void of content. What hammer blow has the person or thing that is lying there received to make it unconscious of anything, stupefied until the moment when memory, flooding back, restores to it consciousness or personality? [II, 271 (II, 891–92)]

The answer to this question, which was the object of the *recherche*, was not found until the end of the novel.

Marcel's thoughts were occupied only occasionally by this metaphysical malaise; his mundane existence tended to suppress such feelings. But the dream, being the seat of both this unity and the truth regarding reality, at times inexorably posed the problem of the unity of the self. Doubts as to the existence of this unity having been raised at the outset, the entire work then traces step by step the course that culminated in a mystical affirmation (based entirely on emotional evidence) of the unity of the self.

Proust does not say in so many words that the origin of Marcel's thirst for unity, of the impulse that spurred the Narrator on relentlessly in his quest for proofs, was the unconscious; however, this is amply demonstrated in dreams:

> it would seem that there is no longer any need for a suggestion or stimulus coming from the conscious self, which, at first glance, seems to be the unique possessor of the sense of unity

and synthesis as well as the desire for permanence. Now the initial urge to resuscitate the "authentic impression" arises, so to speak, in the subconscious; just the same, we can only interpret this initial impulse as a manifestation of the will to survive intact, referred to previously. Such is the dream that revives for the Narrator the memory of Albertine which is on the point of fading forever from his affective memory (here, actually, the variations are such that it is no longer possible to attribute to this dream the indirectly protective function that we attributed to the previous one).... [18]

When in waking life Marcel doubted the reality of his experiences, the unique proof of their concreteness was found in the emotions he felt towards them, whose reality he could not doubt: "And yet this love for Albertine which I felt almost vanish when I attempted to realise it, seemed in a measure to acquire a proof of its existence from the intensity of my grief at this moment" (II, 484 [III, 151]). This was, however, not a proof of exterior reality ("But this renewal of my suffering gave no further consistency to the image that I beheld of Albertine" [II, 484 (III, 152)]); it was only a proof of the permanence of the self that had loved her.

This waking experience was incomplete, whereas the dream was able to revive images of exterior reality because it is outside the infinitesimal divisions of time which prevent the individual from seizing the reality of the present moment as a unified experience.

Memory was the sought-after link between the various disparate selves. If a permanent self can be found at all in the midst of such relentless change, it can only be the phenomenon of memory; thus the memory, as the repository for all the successive selves it stores up (and which it survives), acquires an identity of its own and constitutes the permanent self.[19]

Notes

15. See *La Recherche*, I, 8–9 (II, 91).

16. Pierre-Henri Simon, *Témoins de l'homme* (Paris, Armand Colin, 1955), p. 5.

17. Albert Béguin, *L'Ame romantique et le rêve* (Paris, José Corti, 1939), p. 353.

18. Aulagne, *Psyché*, No. 35–36 (septembre–octobre 1949), 882 (WSB).

19. Blondel, *La Psychographie de Marcel Proust*, p. 61.

—William Stewart Bell, *Proust's Nocturnal Muse* (New York and London: Columbia University Press, 1962): 112–115.

JEAN-FRANÇOIS REVEL ON LOVE'S ILLUSION

[Renowned French journalist and thinker, Jean-François Revel is best known for his political writings, which include *Democracy Against Itself* and *The Totalitarian Temptation*. In this extract, he details the crucial important of self-deception in Proust's narrated love affairs.]

Proust chose the easy way, which was the opposite of what he did in his critique of snobbery, by choosing in Albertine a person who was basically unfaithful and given to sleeping round. His story would have been even finer if he had shown that the phenomena, on which I have tried to summarize his views, had occurred between faithful lovers.

What doubts about himself, what an urge to present himself continually in the most favorable light, to envisage from the very first moment, even before it comes into being, a passion as it *will be* when it reaches the stage of mutual destruction of the lovers! For in the last resort the narrator of *Remembrance of Things Past* is always deceived, or dropped. He is in love with Mme de Guermantes before he meets her and of course without his love being returned. Gilberte and Albertine are girls whom he pursues and who run away from him. There is never any question of his growing tired of anybody except when he has been firmly repulsed. Proust is different in one respect from so many other people; he never shows himself as a person who causes suffering to others, who is loved more than he loves. He displays a great humility, a curious absence of self-esteem in so far as he never for a moment suggests that personal charm could of itself remove from his partners the desire to be unfaithful to him. He is still in need of external methods—a disciplinary framework and good policing. They turn out to be entirely useless in practice. The Proustian mistresses, and not only the narrator's, are simply waiting to be left alone for a couple of minutes in order to "get rid of a passing fancy." The moment you turn your back, they vanish into the toilet with the head waiter. Why does Rachel start "making eyes at a young scholar" in a restaurant? Not simply to annoy Saint-Loup, but (as Proust emphasizes) she often does it with the intention of really meeting the unknown person again later on. But why does she do it on *that particular day*, since Saint-Loup is almost never in Paris, except for the fact that the author wants to return and to link everything up with the universal practice of women *making their escape*: behavior which is quite unnecessary in the present instance because it is only on very rare occasions that Rachel finds herself under Saint-Loup's control?

Proust formulates the principle that one always loves without one's love being returned. That is probably the reason why, in spite of the appalling jealousy from which he suffers, his own love never changes to hate; a description of the dynamism of *amour-passion* which for once differs radically from the Racinian pattern. There is one other thing that Proust has described: in love you can never revenge yourself either because in doing so you would ruin yourself or because you no longer have the least desire to do it. It is true that, as a result of his absence of self-esteem, he never feels the need of revenge. For everywhere in Proust we come across this humility in principle, this basic lack of confidence in himself, this robustly tough attitude which takes for granted that "the women in our lives" can never be anything but prisoners or fugitives while waiting to become indifferent to us.

When they have become indifferent or before our passion starts, it sometimes happens that like Gilberte they "throw themselves at our heads." And apart from *amour-passion*, we ourselves awaken the desires and inclinations, even the beginnings of passion in other people, provided that we do not succumb to it ourselves. Everything turns out as though *amour-passion* at once put the partner to flight, as though passion could only arouse in her non-passion. If one wishes to keep the beloved, it is only out of interest, "benevolence in the most protective sense of the word"—benevolence of the kind that Baron de Charlus displays towards Morel.

There is, to be sure, an element of simplification in this mechanism: when I want you, you don't want me; when you want me, I don't want you. We should probably find some psychological verification of this point in André Roussin or Jean de Létraz. Proust was mistaken in putting forward the view that negation was the only outcome. It is not true that things *always* turn out like that. But according to Proust, even if it is not always like that, it *ought* to be. The real hazard, which is the result of a "coincidence", is that it will turn out differently. The real illusion is that "things will work out" because in essence love, which is said to be shared, in fact continues not to be. It is never anything but a misunderstanding and a lie except perhaps for a very brief moment when, to use an outmoded but exquisite definition of chance, there is the "meeting of two independent series." But Proust differs from Létraz chiefly because the law, which according to him is general, that prompts people to offer themselves to us either too soon or too late and run away when we go after them, is less a matter of circumstance than the fact that it is not at all a question of the same sort of inclination in both cases. If we do not desire a person who appears to offer herself to us, it is precisely because we desire her so little. The same "offer," if the desire became passion, would appear derisory.

The sudden change from the first to the second kind of desire takes place during the celebrated episode of the return by train with Albertine at the end of *Cities of the Plain*. First of all, Albertine is importunate and irritates the narrator; her presence far exceeds his need of her. Then, after the fatal sentence about Mlle Vinteuil, no presence could possibly ever satisfy the passion which explodes. For in fact, in *The Captive*, it is certainly not said that Albertine does not love the narrator. Many lovers would envy them the life they lead. If we place Albertine's infidelities, which are sporadic, beside the complete surrender of her existence, can we say that they are the cause of the narrator's suffering? The fatality which hangs over *The Captive* from the beginning is more essential. The defeat of passion is inevitable: it belongs to its nature. The hunt for and discovery of infidelities is much more an external confirmation. We might say of them, as one says of God and with as many reasons for believing in success, that if they did not exist one would have to invent them. It is not the discovery of the infidelities that brings about the collapse of passion, but a sense of the impossibility of finding happiness in passion, which prompts the search for proofs of infidelity, itself making infidelity inevitable because when it comes to passion who is there who is not unfaithful? The person whom one loves passionately becomes from this very fact unfaithful, always in retreat in face of our madness.

Why? Proust has pointed out that we can be conscious of the lack of interest or the beauty of a person, and still love her and above all suffer from her loss because she plays the part of the liaison officer, the hyphen between ourselves and love, gives us access to a life where love exists, a life which love cleanses of all boredom, a life in which, whatever happens, we are never alone or rather we never feel ourselves alone because the essential fact is the continual *possibility* of communicating with somebody and not the fact of always finding ourselves in her company. Sometimes one may even avoid such company, find it importunate. Yet it remains true that in the depths of our being we are constantly attempting to escape from solitude. And it is, indeed, the announcement of an irremediable solitude which with age will bring that day "which is as sad as a winter night," when the narrator has to admit that money alone and not love will provide him with sexual pleasure for a night with beings "whom he will never see again."

Up to that point, it is not because the object is amiable and loved that love exists, but the object is loved *in order that* love may exist. It follows that in Proust love is not an internal autarchic mechanism whose object would only be a pretext, a screen on to which our subjective obsessions are projected. No doubt this form of projection is never absent from love and the face of the passer-by, whom we might perhaps be able to love, and is sometimes no more than "*un espace vide sur lequel jouerait tout au plus le reflet de nos désirs* (an empty space with nothing more upon it than a flickering reflection of our desires)."[1] But at the same time the desire to love is directed straight towards the exterior; it is a sign of the need to escape from oneself notwithstanding the fact that it is directed less to objective "properties", to "qualities" inherent in the object, than the search for something *by means of the object* and beyond it: the fact of being in love with the object and being loved by it. That is why the beloved is always both an absolute, because she is the only means of access to love, and a collaborator whom one distrusts because an empirical and uncertain individual, with her limitations, her outbursts of temper, her falseness, her versatility, eventually her stupidity and weakness, may not be the ideal collaborator, may even be the worst collaborator possible. That is why she inhabits us completely and is at the same time a stranger to us. At the very moment when her loss would make us suffer a thousand deaths, we find ourselves considering her in everyday life with a sardonic eye and noting down with resignation or irritation her incurable banality. Then, when she has ceased to exist as an object of love, the uncertain individual who remains becomes more distant from us and more indifferent to us than anybody else; we do not even feel for her ultimate destiny the curiosity we feel for our own most distant relations, the vaguest of our friends. It is because our links with the last, however loose they may be, have been established on account of qualities which belong to him independently of his relations with us. The links are therefore the result of sound and lasting reasons, however minor they may be. On the contrary, the individuality which is independent of ourselves to which the loved one returns, collapses for us, when love collapses, into the void.

When Proust receives at Venice the telegram mistakenly signed Albertine, which makes him believe for a moment that she is not dead, he does not feel the least *curiosity* at the prospect of seeing her again, even if it were only for a moment, not because he is afraid of suffering, but out of sheer lack of interest. We are as far away from women whom we no longer love as we are from the dead, as he will repeat in *The Past Recaptured*. Or then, if he wants to see Gilberte again, it is in order to make use of her as a go-between because she can arrange for him to meet girls at her home. This individuality, in fact, in so far as it belongs to a person not loved by us, does not possess, or only does so in exceptional circumstances, any quality which would make us want to see her in preference to thousands of other people.

Therefore the only way of ridding ourselves of a passion, even if it were only beginning, does not consist in verifying, in experiencing once again, its intolerable character, but in avoiding all actual contact with the object, in ensuring that it is physically absent even when it is affectively present because the less often it uses that property of its body which acts as a conductor of the sentiment of love, the more rapidly it will lose it. It is the only case in Proust in which time exercises a day to day influence. It is necessary to treasure the time of separation. It is the result of the force of fact and not of reason, or even of feeling, that we cease to love.

Thus the beloved object is not a beloved object, but a means of loving. The Proustian conception of love, in which people have seen a banal skepticism which reduces passion to a fortuitous psychological phenomenon, is related on the contrary to the Platonic vision. On one side there are carnal beings who are numerous and changing; beyond them there is an eternal object of love which is incorruptible and permanent. But it is only through the first that we can take cognizance of the second. "*Chaque sentiment particulier est une partie de l'universel amour* (Each particular feeling is a tiny fragment of the universal love)."[2] As in art, the individual object awakens our longing for a durable and precious reality. Like the three trees at Hudimesnil, it serves as a gesture of appeal; it is a flash from a kingdom still buried even more deeply in us than memory; a kingdom that not even memory can restore to us. Such is the great difference between the lesson drawn from the impression one gets in front of the three trees at Hudimesnil and the analyses of the sensations evoked by the *madeleine* or the unequal paving stones of the Quai Conti.

But Plato himself believed in the actual existence of a world which transcended physical beings. Carnal beauty and the beauty of works of art may fall back into the state of becoming and into oblivion; they have fulfilled their function as intermediate stages; their fall is the start of the deliverance of the spirit. In Proust, who does not believe in any form of transcendence, their annihilation is irremediable. This accounts for the haunting sensation which causes the shadows of love to dodge in and out among people like the ferret of the song, like letters of credit which pass from hand to hand and are used to pay for twenty purchases without anybody ever cashing them or, owing to lack of provision, being able to cash them.[3] Certain people, who are responsible for coining the idea of universal love, possess the same faculty that we find in Plato for suggesting the taste of an absolute which does not belong to their imperfect and flighty nature. In reality, they have only themselves to offer, but at the same time they inspire the desire for much more than themselves and reveal their inability to satisfy the need which they arouse. That is why love is identified with suffering. No person is lovable in himself. They are all lovable because they can all inspire the love of a Sovereign Good which surpasses them. But in Proust the Sovereign Good (*le Souverain Bien*) does not exist. With him a meticulously empirical intelligence in the service of a mystical sensibility refuses out of a concern for truth to grant this sensibility the illusory satisfaction which it demands imperiously. It would have been easy to deal differently with things. It would have been easy to write: "You would not seek me if you had not already found me." It would have been easy to hurry along once again and in the wake of so many other people, and either as a philosopher to extract the positive from the negative, knowledge from ignorance, hope from despair; or as an artist to draw from this very despair lovely mirages which can create the lasting illusion that it stands for the opposite of what it really is. He records the contradiction of human life. Where he shows himself skeptical, it is not through insensibility and he does not deny the existence of a need which is impossible to satisfy, but when he feels the need of an absolute joy he does not conclude that the object of this joy is bound to exist under one form or another in order to satisfy us. It emerges that man is tortured by a desire for objects which do not exist. It is like that, and that is all there is to it.

Notes

1. III, p. 1045; *The Past Recaptured*: p. 270 (RH); p. 469 (C&W).

2. II, p. 120; *The Guermantes Way*: I, p. 800 (RH); V, p. 158 (C&W).

3. For a good example of the ferret course, see III, p. 984; *The Past Recaptured*, p. 221 (RH); p. 385 (C&W).

—Jean-François Revel, *On Proust* (New York: The Library Press, 1972): 93–100.

Gérard Genette on the Duration of the Narrative

[Gérard Genette, formerly of the Ecole des Hautes Etudes en Science Sociales, in Paris, was one of the most important later structuralist critics. His best-known works include *Fiction and Diction*, and *Paratexts: Thresholds of Interpretation*. In this passage, he discusses the relationship of narrative and time.]

The narrating instance of the *Recherche* obviously corresponds to this last type. We know that Proust spent more than ten years writing his novel, but Marcel's act of narrating bears no mark of duration, or of division: it is instantaneous. The narrator's present, which on almost every page we find mingled with the hero's various pasts, is a single moment without progression. Marcel Muller thought he found in Germaine Brée the hypothesis of a double narrating instance—before and after the final revelation—but this hypothesis has no basis, and in fact all I see in Germaine Brée is an improper (although common) use of "narrator" for *hero*, which perhaps led Muller into error on that point.[32] As for the feelings expressed on the final pages of *Swann*, which we know do not correspond to the narrator's final conviction, Muller himself shows very well that they do not at all prove the existence of a narrating instance prior to the revelation;[33] on the contrary, the letter to Jacques Rivière quoted above[34] shows that Proust was anxious to tune the narrator's discourse to the hero's "errors," and thus to impute to the narrator a belief not his own, in order to avoid disclosing his own mind too early. Even the narrative Marcel produces after the

Guermantes soirée, the narrative of his beginnings as a writer (seclusion, rough drafts, first reactions of readers), which necessarily takes into account the length of writing ("like him too, ... I had something to write. But my task was longer than his, my words had to reach more than a single person. My task was long. By day, the most I could hope for was to try to sleep. If I worked, it would be only at night. But I should need many nights, a hundred perhaps, or even a thousand")[35] and the interrupting fear of death—even this narrative does not gainsay the fictive instantaneousness of its narrating: for the book Marcel then begins to write *in the story* cannot legitimately be identified with the one Marcel has then almost finished writing *as narrative*—and which is the *Recherche* itself. Writing the fictive book, which is the subject of the narrative, is, like writing every book, a "task [that] was long." But the actual book, the narrative-book, does not have knowledge of its own "length": it does away with its own duration.

The present of Proustian narrating—from 1909 to 1922—corresponds to many of the "presents" of the writing, and we know that almost a third of the book—including, as it happens, the final pages—was written by 1913. The fictive moment of narrating has thus *in fact* shifted in the course of the real writing; today it is no longer what it was in 1913, at the moment when Proust thought his work concluded for the Grasset edition. Therefore, the temporal intervals he had in mind—and wanted to signify—when he wrote, for example apropos of the bedtime scene, "Many years have passed since that night," or apropos of the resurrection of Combray by the madeleine, "I can measure the resistance, I can hear the echo of great spaces traversed"—these spaces have increased by more than ten years simply because the story's time has lengthened: the signified of these sentences is no longer the same. Whence certain irreducible contradictions like this one: the narrator's *today* is obviously, for us, later than the war, but the "Paris today" of the last pages of *Swann* remains in its historical determinations (its referential content) a prewar Paris, as it was seen and described in its better days. The novelistic *signified* (the moment of the narrating) has become something like 1925, but the historical *referent*, which corresponds to the moment of the writing, did not keep pace and continues to say: 1913. Narrative analysis must register these shifts—and the resulting discordances—as effects of the actual genesis of the work; but in the end analysis can look at the narrating instance only as it is given in the final state of the text, as a single moment without duration, necessarily placed several years after the last "scene," therefore after the war, and even, as we have seen,[36] after the death of Marcel Proust. This paradox, let us remember, is not one: Marcel is not Proust, and nothing requires him to die with Proust. What is required, on the other hand, is that Marcel spend "many years" after 1916 in a clinic, which necessarily puts his return to Paris and the Guermantes matinée in 1921 at the earliest, and the meeting with an Odette "showing signs of senility" in 1923.[37] That consequence is a must.

Between this single narrating instant and the different moments of the story, the interval is necessarily variable. If "many years" have elapsed since the bedtime scene in Combray, it is only "of late" that the narrator has again begun to hear his childhood sobs, and the interval separating the narrating instant from the Guermantes matinée is obviously smaller than the interval separating narrating instant and the hero's first arrival in Balbec. The system of language, the uniform use of the past tense, does not allow this gradual shrinking to be imprinted in the very texture of the narrative discourse, but we have seen that to a certain extent Proust had succeeded in making it felt, by modifications in the temporal pacing of the narrative: gradual disappearance of the iterative, lengthening of the singulative scenes, increasing discontinuity, accentuation of the rhythm—as if the story time were tending to dilate and make itself more and more conspicuous while drawing near its end, *which is also its origin*.

According to what we have already seen to be the common practice of "autobiographical" narrating, we could expect to see the narrative bring its hero to the point where the narrator awaits him, in order that these two hypostases might meet and finally merge. People have sometimes, a little quickly, claimed that this is what happens.[38] In fact, as Marcel Muller well notes, "between the day of the reception at the Princess's and the day when the Narrator recounts that reception there extends a whole era which maintains a gap between the Hero and the Narrator, a gap that cannot be bridged: the verbal forms in the conclusion of the *Temps retrouvé* are all in the past tense."[39] The narrator brings his hero's story—his own story—precisely to the point when, as Jean Rousset says, "the hero is about to become the narrator";[40] I would say rather, is *beginning to become* the narrator, since he actually starts in on his writing. Muller writes that "if the Hero overtakes the Narrator, it is like an asymptote: the interval separating them approaches zero, but will never reach it," but his image connotes a Sterneian play on the two durations that does not in fact exist in Proust. There is simply the narrative's halt at the point when the hero has discovered the truth and the meaning of his life: at the point, therefore, when this "story of a vocation"—which, let us remember, is the avowed subject of Proustian narrative—comes to an end. The rest, whose outcome is already known to us by the very novel that concludes here, no longer belongs to the "vocation" but to the effort that follows it up, and must therefore be only sketched in. The subject of the *Recherche* is indeed "Marcel becomes a writer," not "Marcel the writer": the *Recherche* remains a novel of development, and to see it as a "novel about the novelist," like the *Faux Monnayeurs* [*The Counterfeiters*], would be to distort its intentions and above all to violate its meaning; it is a novel about the future novelist. "The continuation," Hegel said, precisely apropos of the Bildungsroman, "no longer has anything novelistic about it." Proust probably would have been glad to apply that formulation to his own narrative: what is novelistic is the quest, the *search* [*recherche*], which ends at the discovery (the revelation), not at the use to which that discovery will afterward be put. The final discovery of the truth, the late encounter with the vocation, like the happiness of lovers reunited, can be only a denouement, not an interim stopping place; and in this sense, the subject of the *Recherche* is indeed a traditional subject. So it is necessary that the narrative be interrupted before the hero overtakes the narrator; it is inconceivable for them both together to write: The End. The narrator's last sentence is when—is *that*—the hero finally reaches his first. The interval between the end of the story and the moment of the narrating is therefore the time it takes the hero to write this book, which is and is not the book the narrator, in his turn, reveals to us in a moment brief as a flash of lightning.

Notes

32. Muller, p. 45; Germaine Brée, *Marcel Proust and Deliverance from Time*, trans. C. J. Richards and A. D. Truitt, 2d ed. (New Brunswick, N.J., 1969), pp. 19–20.

33. Muller, p. 46.

34. Pp. 199–200.

35. RH II, 1136/P III, 1043.

36. P. 91.

37. This episode takes place (RH II, 1063/P III, 951) "Less than three years"—thus more than two years—after the Guermantes matinée.

38. In particular Louis Martin-Chauffier: "As in memoirs, the man who writes and the man whose life we see are distinct in time, but tend to catch up with each other in the long run; they are moving towards the day when the progress of the hero through his life stops at the table, where the narrator, no longer separated from him in time nor tied to him by memory, invites him to sit down beside him so that both together may write: the End" ("Proust and the Double I," *Partisan Review*, 16 [October 1949], 1012).

39. Muller, pp. 49–50. Let us remember, however, that certain anticipations (like the last meeting with Odette) cover a part of that "era."

40. Rousset, p. 144.

—Gérard Genette, *Narrative Discourse: An Essay in Method*, (Ithaca, New York: Cornell University Press, 1980): 223–227.

PLOT SUMMARY OF

Swann's Way

In the initial section, designated the "overture" by translators, Marcel considers the matter of sleep and dreaming, the mysterious wandering associations of half-sleep. Not only does this passage draw our attention to all that is present but not fully available to our consciousness at any given time, it also establishes that the act of reading itself is something like dreaming. Furthermore, just as dreams and half-conscious thought follow lines of association rather than strictly linear or formal patterns, so the novel that is to unfold here will zig-zag back and forth through time and space, following Marcel's own particular associations.

As a child, Marcel was unable to fall asleep without a good-night kiss from his mother. On one occasion, during a visit from Charles Swann (whose own story will occupy half of *Swann's Way*), his mother is unable to come upstairs to his bedroom. Marcel grows so preoccupied with his desire for his mother's kiss that he realizes he will not be able to sleep without it, and sends their servant, Françoise, down to his mother with a note asking her to come up. Eventually, after Swann has gone, his mother and father ascend the stairs only to encounter young Marcel waiting. His mother is irritated with him, but his father, the prospect of whose disapproval terrifies Marcel, simply suggests that his mother sleep in Marcel's room that night, so as not to leave him alone at all. This episode, though trivial enough to an adult observer, is realized with all the strong emotion of childhood, and Marcel remarks on the rather arbitrary way in which his father made decisions regarding him.

Moving forward into the more recent present, Marcel describes another apparently mundane, but actually deeply significant incident. He happens to eat a madeleine soaked in tea, and the flavor gives rise in him to a strange, ghostly sensation. After pondering on it for a while, he remembers how, as a boy, growing up in the small town of Combray, he had been given madeleines soaked in tea by his invalid Aunt Léonie. That particular flavor, not tasted again until this episode, revives in Marcel memories he had been certain were "all dead." The next section of the novel, entitled "Combray," emerges complete from this moment of involuntary memory, a phenomenon that will reoccur throughout the novel.

"Combray" consists of Marcel's boyhood memories; we meet his bedridden Aunt Léonie and her religiose friend Eulalie, and a number of characters who will play important roles later on have walk-on moments here. Marcel happens to run across his Uncle Adolphe in the company of a mysterious woman in pink, whose name he does not learn. Later, he will learn that she was Odette de Crécy, Swann's future wife, and the mother of his first love, Gilberte. Later on, he will see her again, walking with a dapper man later revealed to be the Baron de Charlus. Near Combray, there are two paths, one of which runs by Swann's house and is thus called Swann's Way; the other, which runs by the country home of the rich and high-status Duc and Duchesse de Guermantes, is called the Guermantes Way. The young Marcel is fascinated with the aristocracy, and at one point catches sight of the Duchesse de Guermantes, sitting in her family's pew in the church at Combray, and illuminated by the light of a stained-glass window in which her own ancestors are depicted.

Only in "Swann in Love," the next section, does Proust expand the point of view of the novel beyond Marcel's own experiences. Here he recounts Swann's love affair with Odette in the third person, offering the reader Swann's, and even briefly Odette's, thoughts and feelings. Normally, Marcel presents his characters purely as he observes them socially, allowing them to reveal themselves gradually, rather than simply telling the reader all about them.

Swann is introduced to Odette by a friend, who thinks they might perhaps take to each other. Swann finds Odette to be the precise opposite of his type, and slightly shallow as well. He spends time with her, but without interest. Through her, he is introduced to the Verdurins.

Like all important people in French society, the Guermantes maintain a salon of socially prominent persons, artists, and some professionals. Aristocratic salons such as these are aped by lesser, bourgeois persons like Monsieur and Madame Verdurin, who maintain a constant presence throughout *In Search of Lost Time*. Swann, whose circle of friends and acquaintances includes the cream of French society, and the Prince of Wales, is something of a catch for them. During his first visit to the Verdurins, Swann sits beside Odette as a sonata by the fictional composer Vinteuil, is played. Transported by the music, he begins to associate the exalted feelings it gives him with Odette. Later, this mingling of art and love will be further extended when Swann notices Odette's resemblance to the daughter of Jethro in a painting by Botticelli. One evening, on arriving later than usual at the Verdurins, he discovers that Odette has already departed, and finds himself powerfully affected. He searches for her in the streets without success, and is forced to the conclusion that he has fallen in love with her.

Swann declares his love for her, and she becomes his mistress. In an inversion of expectations typical of Proust, Swann is perhaps the only person in Paris who is unaware of Odette's promiscuity with lovers of both sexes, and that she is a rather simpleminded, and even vulgar, person. Making a point that will be repeated throughout *In Search of Lost Time*, Proust indicates that, after the initial infatuation has dwindled, the most powerful emotion in love is jealousy. Swann quickly comes to doubt Odette's honesty and fidelity, and suspects her of carrying on at least flirtation with Forcheville, another member of the Verdurin circle. One night, after leaving Odette at her apartment, he returns secretly, hoping to catch her with him; however, he knocks on the wrong window and flees the scene in embarrassment. Later the reader will learn that, had Swann knocked on Odette's window that night, he would have discovered her with Forcheville. Swann meanwhile finds his proof: a letter from Odette to Forcheville, which he is able to make out through the thin envelope.

The Verdurins have observed the romance between Swann and Odette with growing interest. Unconsciously resenting Swann's superior taste and social connections, Mme Verdurin expels him from her circle. Momentarily thrust outside of society, or at least this corner of it, and made extremely observant and reflective by his jealousy, Swann begins to fall out of love with Odette. In a dream, he sees her as she first appeared to him, rather stupid and not at all his type, and realizes that he had loved a phantom of his own creation all along.

In the final section, "Place-Names: The Name," the reader returns to Marcel's boyhood narrative. The title of the section refers to a long meditation about travel and the mystique of far-away places, which is consistent with his theme of the glamour of distant things and persons. Balbec, which he will visit in the next volume, has a special mystique for him; a seaside Norman town he imagines to be a purely untouched medieval relic. He will of course be disappointed.

However, ill-health prevents him from travelling. Marcel's doctor suggests that he take regular walks in the Champs-Elysée, to improve his health. There, he encounters a redheaded girl who turns out to be Gilberte Swann. Although he had fallen out of love with Odette, Swann has married her just the same, and Gilberte is their child. Gradually, they become friends, and Marcel falls in love with Gilberte. He describes how anxiously he observed the developments in the weather, since any inclemency would force him to remain home. As with the incident of the good-night kiss, Marcel is again forced to wait to see the one he loves, and the delays and difficulties keeping them apart serve only to increase his desire, his need, for her. They play childish games together, almost always with other children, but on one occasion, a freakishly warm day in winter, they play together alone. Gilberte informs him shortly thereafter that she will be going away for some time, apparently taking poorly-concealed pleasure in tormenting him. In time, Marcel will discover that "In my friendship with Gilberte, it was I alone who loved." *Swann's Way* ends with Marcel's discovery that Odette and Swann are married, and with a melancholy reminiscence about the Bois de Boulogne, the artificial Parisian gardens in which Odette, now Mme Swann, walks with other fashionable women.

LIST OF CHARACTERS IN *Swann's Way*

"Marcel" the anonymous narrator, a middle-aged man looking back on his childhood. A sensitive, intelligent, literary, somewhat selfish boy.

Marcel's mother finds her son somewhat too clinging and dependent, but who is one of the few prominent characters in the novel without significant flaws.

Marcel's father is a distant figure who plays little role in Marcel's life. He has great power to affect his son, but applies it inconsistently and distractedly.

Marcel's grandmother is perhaps the only figure in *In Search of Lost Time* who is not depicted as ultimately selfish. She has her "principles," which include regular walks in the garden, even in the rain, and keeping her husband from drinking brandy at any cost.

Marcel's grandfather is a knowing old man who takes great pleasure in mischieviously disobeying and upsetting his wife.

Françoise is the family servant, who will attend Marcel throughout the novel. A hard woman, capable of great sympathy for the sufferings of those in far-away places and oblivious to the suffering of those around her.

Odette de Crécy, later Odette Swann; a promiscuous, bisexual high-society courtesan, affecting a certain poise and sophistication, but a basically selfish, shallow, unintelligent woman.

Charles Swann is an exemplar of elegant taste and exquisite manners, aesthetic judgement and lofty, but unostentatious, intellect. He will fall incongruously in love with Odette de Crécy, and eventually marries her.

Gilberte Swann is the daughter of Charles and Odette Swann. A pretty, redheaded girl with a tendency to be flighty. Enjoys her first experience of the power that another's love gives her.

Aunt Léonie, Marcel's invalid aunt in Combray, out of whose cup of tea the entire boyhood section grows. A kind, pious woman.

Eulalie, Aunte Léonie's friend, who comes to visit her daily. Her affectations of piety cover a spiteful personality.

Vinteuil's daughter, unnamed young woman, whose father, the composer Vinteuil, wrote the sonata which becomes the "national anthem" of Swann's love for Odette. Young Marcel secretly observes her with her female lover.

Madame Verdurin maintains a middlebrow bourgeois salon, which serves to bring Odette and Swann together. A calculating, hypocritical woman with no real sensitivity to art.

Monsieur Verdurin is Mme Verdurin's overbearing, slightly ogrish husband, who is likewise more concerned with his social standing than with the high art and culture he affects to understand.

Bergotte is young Marcel's literary idol. While he does not turn out to be the elegant figure Marcel imagined him to be, Bergotte, though somewhat rough of manner, is an unusually perceptive and intelligent man.

Doctor Cottard, comically vapid hanger-on with the Verdurins. A quack who mistakenly believes himself to be the soul of wit, constantly interjecting into other people's conversations with corny puns and lame quotations.

Bloch, hyper-sensitive young Jewish student, constantly making social gaffes. He speaks in an overly-elaborate, literary manner that is clearly meant to cover his insecurities about being accepted. Possibly a caricature of Proust himself.

Forcheville, Odette's haughty lover, from the Verdurin circle. A pompous, insulting man.

CRITICAL VIEWS OF
Swann's Way

J. MIDDLETON MURRY ON THE EPOCH OF *SWANN'S WAY*

[Founder of the avant-garde literary magazine *Rhythm* in the late 1900s, J. Middleton Murry's articles also appeared in the *Nation* and the *Westminster Gazette*. Author of many critical books and articles, including *Fyodor Dostoevsky* and *The Problem of Style*, he is best known for his study, *Keats and Shakespeare*. In this extract from an essay written a year after Proust's death, Murry discusses the relationship between *Swann's Way* and the contemporary epoch, with particular attention to the question of whether or not *Swann's Way* is the last gasp of an old sensibility or the first appearance of a new one.]

At the beginning of *Du Côté de chez Swann* he had been at pains to give us not merely his results but his method also. He was a grown man, suddenly waking from sleep, trying to locate himself once more in his room, and his room in the world; and something familiar in this strange sensation had reminded him of his sensations in his bedroom as a child. But "reminded" is altogether too coarse and summary a word for the delicate process on which his researches depended; rather it is that a familiarity in the strange sensation whispers to him that it holds a secret for him if he will only explore it. It conceals something that he must know. Again, it is the vague familiarity of the faint flavour of a *madeleine* dipped in tea, which the grown man is eating in his mother's company, which ultimately yields up the magnificently vivid picture of Combray and Aunt Léonie. These sensations, or presentiments of the past, come to the boy also. There is, for example, the beautiful account of his mysterious excitement at a sight of the spire and towers of Martinville church when he is driving home in Dr. Percepied's carriage. Again he has the sense of memories he cannot grasp, of a secret and mystical message that he cannot make his own; it is the occasion of his first attempt at writing.[1] These premonitions become more frequent during his stay with his grandmother at the Balbec hotel. Then the sudden sight of a tiny clump of trees seen while he is driving with the Marquise de Villeparisis makes him feel that they are stretching out imploring arms towards him in a mute appeal. If he can divine what they have to tell him (they seem to say) he will touch the secret of "la vraie vie," of life indeed. And then the writer warns us that the story of his search to make this secret his own is to come, and that this premonition of a task to be accomplished was to haunt him throughout his life.

At this moment Marcel Proust came nearest, we may believe, to revealing to the reader the hidden soul of his own book. There is room for different interpretations, of course, and it is admitted that in any case he was frequently distracted from whatever plan he had by his delight in a pure description of the human comedy from the angle most familiar to him. Nevertheless, we are persuaded that Proust brought to the exact and intimate analysis of his own sensations something more than the self-consciousness of talent—some element, let us say, of an almost religious fervour. This modern of the moderns, this *raffiné* of *raffinés*, had a mystical strain in his composition. These hidden messages of a moment these glimpses and intuitions of "la vraie vie" behind a veil, were of the utmost importance to him; he had some kind of immediate certainty of their validity. He confessed as much, and we are entitled to take a man so reticent at his word.

We may take him at his word also when he acknowledges that the effort to penetrate behind the veil of these momentary perceptions was the chief interest of his life. The first of these illuminations—the vision of Martinville spire—had taken shape in a piece of writing which he gives us. We suspect that the last did also, and that its visible expression is the whole series of volumes which, after all, do bear a significant title—*A la Recherche du Temps Perdu*; we suspect that the last page of the last volume would have brought us to the first page of the first, and that the long and winding narrative would finally have revealed itself as the history of its own conception. Then, we may imagine, all the long accounts of the Guermantes' parties and the extraordinary figure of M. de Charlus would have fallen into their places in the scheme, as part of the surrounding circumstances whose pressure drove the youth and the man into the necessity of discovering a reality within himself. What he was to discover, when the demand that he should surrender himself to his moments of vision became urgent and finally irresistible, was the history of what he was. Proust—and amid the most labyrinthine of his complacent divagations into the *beau monde* a vague sense of this attends us—was much more than a sentimental autobiographer of genius; he was a man trying to maintain his soul alive. And thus, it may be, we have an explanation of the rather surprising fact that he began his work so late. The two volumes which went before *Du Côté de chez Swann*[2] were not indeed negligible, but they were the work of a dilettante. The explanation, we believe, is that in spite of his great gifts Proust was a writer *malgré lui*; he composed against the grain. We mean that had it been only for the sake of the satisfaction of literary creation, he probably would not have written at all. It was only when writing presented itself to him as the only available means for getting down to the bedrock of his own personality, as the only instrument by which his *fin-de-siècle* soul—the epithet is, in his case, a true definition—could probe to something solid to live by, that he seriously took up the pen. It was the lance with which he rode after the Grail—"la vraie vie."

Proust at the first glance looks wholly different from a man who rides off on a desperate adventure. There seems to be no room for desperate adventures in the Faubourg Saint-Germain. It is hardly congruous to some senses to ride through the waste land in a sixty horse-power limousine. Nevertheless, it can be done. The outward and visible sign is, not for the first time, different from the inward and spiritual grace.

So by a devious path we return to our first question. Proust marks an epoch. What kind of epoch? Is it an end or a beginning? And the answer we have reached is the answer we might have expected in the case of a figure so obviously considerable. Proust is both an end and a beginning. More an end than a beginning, perhaps, if we have regard to the technique and texture of his work. In the art of literature itself he opens up no new way. And, in the deeper sense, he indicates a need more than he satisfies it. The modern mind, looking into the astonishing mirror which Proust holds up to it, will not see in it the gleam of something to live by; but it will see, if it knows how to look, an acknowledgement of that necessity and a burning desire to satisfy it. By so much Marcel Proust marks a beginning also. It is the flame of this desire which smoulders always through his book, and at times breaks out; it is this which makes it his own, and this which gives it, in the true sense, style.

NOTES

1. In another and rather complicated sense this is a presentiment of the future. The spires appear to have been those of Caen, the carriage a motor car, the year evidently much later. The original article will be found in *Pastiches et Mélanges*, on pp. 91 to 99—C. K. S. M.

2. I.e., *Les Plaisirs et les Jours*, published in 1896, and *Pastiches et Mélanges*, which, strictly speaking, did not come as a volume until after *A l'Ombre des Jeunes Filles en Fleurs*, in the spring of 1919. But of the *Pastiches* some at least had appeared in the *Figaro* in 1908 and 1909, while the *Mélanges* date even further, and include the introductions to Proust's translations of Ruskin, *La Bible d'Amiens* (1904) and *Sésame et les Lys* (1906)—C. K. S. M.

—J. Middleton Murry, from *Marcel Proust – An English Tribute*, (collected by C. K. Scott Moncrieff, New York: Thomas Seltzer, 1923): 106–110.

MILTON L. MILLER ON NOSTALGIA IN *SWANN'S WAY*

[Milton L. Miller was one of the charter members of the North Carolina Psychoanalytic Society, and wrote extensively on psychoanalysis and literature. In this excerpt, he offers a psychological interpretation of Proust's fascination with, and need for, the past.]

The actual story of *Swann's Way*, which is the history of Swann's love affair, is approached by circumlocutions and digressions, followed by detailed unburdening. At first it is Swann's little daughter, Gilberte, who attracts and frustrates the child Marcel. But then we are plunged back in time into a moving account of how Charles Swann, a man of sophisticated taste and high social standing (a successful Jewish stockbroker, beloved by the aristocracy), falls in love with Odette, a courtesan, his inferior socially and intellectually. "To cattleya," meaning to make love, a verb which Proust formed from the name of an orchid, is added to our language by Swann's story. Swann humiliates himself through participation in the meetings of the Verdurin clan, a group of bourgeois social climbers. Madame Verdurin utilizes her wealth to insinuate herself and her adherents into the hub of the fashionable art world and to manipulate whatever aristocratic social "lions" she can attract; thus she exerts a real influence on artistic fashions. Swann spends every evening with this group, only because Odette is to be found in their company. The more completely his passion for Odette absorbs him, the less Odette responds to him. He goes through all the stages of falling in love, from initial indifference to tantalizing rejections by Odette which make him increasingly anxious to hold her affection. We experience his jealousy, his suspicions about being betrayed, his spying on her house at night, and opening her mail—his acquiescence to the knowledge that successful rivals exist, among women as well as men—his abject acceptance of ostracism from the Verdurin clan and his hopeless longing for a woman who is his inferior.

But Swann is a wealthy man, and apparently Odette has decided to marry him for the sake of financial security and social position. After he has outgrown his love he has married her in order to legitimize his daughter; for, at the end of this volume, we see him introduced as Odette's husband and the father of Gilberte Swann. Odette Swann's promenades in the Bois de Boulogne are made especially real for us, by the attractiveness of her person and garments. Children play games in the park, where Odette long ago was seduced by a woman. The men with whom Odette has had affairs watch her walk by, a showy, fascinating figure—for each of them she has a different sort of smile.

Comparing "Marcel" of the novel (and also many aspects of

Swann and other characters) with Proust's actual life, we see that we have here a reconstructed self, such as each human being carries about within him to some extent, in which the romanticized notion of the varied facets of his real personality, and an awareness of the real life within him, is partly composed of drastic departures from fact. There are composites, rather than identical copies of persons and places, in all our inner, subjective lives. Proust's confessions convey emotional reality, one might say, in preference to factual reality. He had the capacity to create a variety of characters with an intimacy composed partly of similar experience and based on an exceptional ability to observe others—and to control feelings in the reader.

After reading *Swann's Way*, one is struck by the idea of sexual urges as the factor that separates one from protected situations. Starting at the beginning of *Swann's Way*, for example, we see that Swann is received into the household of Marcel at Combray only without his wife, who, having been notorious for her promiscuity, is beneath their station. Marcel's mother, grandmother, and great-aunt order Swann about, and do not even thank him directly for the case of Asti wine he has sent them. Françoise, the servant, is equally fastidious, in her way, and prefers to visit her daughter when her son-in-law is absent. Exclusion is one of the main preoccupations of the Verdurin clan, and it is Madame Verdurin who really separates Swann and Odette when they are most in love. Originally it is Swann, the dinner guest, who keeps Marcel's mother away from him at the boy's bedtime. And it is Marcel, sobbing and sick, who prevents his mother and father, the latter already in nightshirt, from retiring together. Jealousy, separating the beloved woman from all other loves—and being separated—are repeated endlessly, but never monotonously, so ingenious are the variations.

Proust's use of imagery never seems accidental. Therefore we must pay attention, in the first pages, when Françoise, the servant, is putting Marcel to bed and Marcel tells us, "For things which might or might not be done she possessed a code at once imperious, abundant, subtle and uncompromising on points themselves imperceptible or irrelevant which gave it a resemblance to those ancient laws which combine such cruel ordinances as the massacre of infants at the breast with prohibitions, of exaggerated refinement, against 'seething the kid in his mother's milk' or 'eating of the sinew which is upon the hollow of the thigh.'" This, in order to show Françoise's obstinacy, is part of the explanation of how difficult it was to get Françoise to summon Mamma, at night when she had guests, to come upstairs to kiss Marcel goodnight. It is one of the rare references to an infant, or nursing, in all the published work of Proust.[2] There is a sadistic connotation in each of the rare instances where he mentions anything connected with infants or birth. (It is always Marcel himself who must be favored, as if in infantile omnipotence.)

Although it is through the taste of the madeleine dipped in tea that Marcel remembers Combray, it is through odors that he recaptures the past most realistically. His curiosity, turned back in time, runs a gamut from the most primitive aspects of his sense of smell to scientific curiosity, aesthetic analysis, and philosophical inquiry. Proust was master of the entire range of curiosity, perceptive even to the degree of trying to cultivate a new sense which might evoke repressed sensations. In *Swann's Way*, we see Marcel's curiosity as that of an eternal child. It was said of the author, when he was an adult, at the time his mother died, that he was still like a four-year-old. To the end of his life, Marcel Proust was referred to by his friends as "le petit Marcel." The power of his curiosity from primitive senses to his aesthetic and intellectual approach, which was the quest for truth, dominates the complete novel.

Typically boyish memories of play with other boys are not mentioned in this volume, which explores so vividly the charm of Combray, and the love affair of Swann, and Marcel's miniature love affair with his mother. It is as if the author were telling us how he found the one acceptable way to assimilate all the tormenting, forbidden loves and hates which beset his boyhood, his confusions in regard to human bodily relationships, masculine competition, and the helplessness that accompanies illness, and his uncertainties about religion and social castes. His solution was to follow the lines his mother laid down, in the direction of literature, and the manipulation of imaginary projections of himself, in beautiful language and artistic forms.

NOTE

2. *Swann's Way*, p. 34.

—Milton L. Miller, *Nostalgia: A Psychoanalytic Study of Marcel Proust*, (Boston: Houghton Mifflin, 1956): 28–31.

GEORGES PIROUÉ ON THE YEARNING FOR ONE WHO IS ABSENT

[In this extract, Piroué discusses the good-night kiss in terms of Proust's characterization of yearning for one who is absent or unavailable.]

Scarcely have we been installed, under the protective covering of night and lowered lids, in the little room at Combray, than something happens. Time lost has made a renewed incursion into time regained. Thanks to it, everything becomes porous. It makes and unmakes, it softens the rigid and opens a door on to the unexpected. The characters of the book are no longer, within the glass walls of a reliquary, mere objects of memory, but flesh and blood to which life has returned, are people in whom the processes of existence have left their mark, their cracks, the growing evidences of decrepitude. The narrator becomes two persons. Proust the maker of his book gives birth to Proust the victim of existence, who, in the shadow of his creative other self, moves painfully along the road which leads to maturity.

Banished from the dining-room, the boy lies waiting for his mother's kiss which alone will make it possible for him to go to sleep. But his mother does not come. In the vacuum created by her absence, the boy's desire grows, becomes ever more complex, takes complete possession of his body and of all his mental and emotional faculties, so that when, at last, two lips are set upon his tear-stained cheek, they no longer bring to him the satisfaction of a whim, but sanctify a love, and extend to it the freedom of the city.

The essence of the narrator's emotional psychology is contained in this anecdote. It is marked, first and foremost, by a sense of the omnipotence of woman. Is not this, the first woman in his life, made "indispensable by the simple fact of having given birth to him"? Even before he has her at his side and can quench his thirst on her presence the boy knows that there exists a being between whom and himself the language of a kiss can abolish loneliness and dispense a total and undifferentiated sense of bliss. Belief in this communion precedes all conscious desire. It is a memory of the time when, as yet unformed and unequipped with the antennae of the senses, he was already loved, before ever wanting to be, within the darkness of the womb. Love is the form taken by a longing for that paradise from which the act of birth has driven him.

It is thus that the mother, and, with her, other women, are known to us from all eternity. We renew our contact with them when, after leaving us upon the threshold of existence, they return to us from all four corners of the horizon, enter into communion with our as yet blinded flesh, and awaken in it a world of obscure reminiscence. Love is possible to us because we already have of it a prenatal experience which life gives us the daily opportunity of verifying. The drama is played out between out visceral memory and the circumstances of life, between the coherence of our own desire, and the incoherence, sometimes auspicious, of the desires of others. Everything happens as though reality, concentrating upon ourselves, were experimenting with different chance combinations, one of which, perhaps, will some day turn out to be adapted to our individual sensibilities. When that moment comes, the door opens, the dream-woman and the living woman melt into one, and our former life coincides with our actual life of the moment.

In just such a way does the narrator remember Gilberte in a garden, making to him a mysterious and conspiratorial sign, the girl of the 'little band' insolently jumping over the old gentleman on the sands, the woman of the dairy in the dark recesses of her shop, the female cyclist in the Bois offering herself to the imaginative glances of the passer-by. In just such a way, too, does Albertine sometimes consent to identify herself with that image of her which he carries in his consciousness. During the period of her long "captivity" there are evenings when she slips her tongue between the young man's lips, like a slice of "daily bread" or "a sacramental wafer to carry him safely through the night". Separated from her own family, and, by the fact of her intrusion, destructive of a family not her own, stripped of her civil status, and as though already dead to society, she is no more than an object of life-giving flesh repeating those antique rites of suckling which are none the less effective for being profane parodies. At other times she sleeps, and then it is that her double, rising to the surface from deep in her lover's consciousness, furtively adjusts its immaterial form to her empty and insensitive body.

Merely in appearance is the narrator's life a worldly one. With his every sense exposed and sniffing the wind, he dreams only of recovering those moments. Something crouching motionless at the centre of his being is ceaselessly engaged in deciphering the hieroglyphics of such human bodies as come within his field of vision, in putting together the fragments of allusive messages, in sounding the nature of intentions. On seashores and in drawing-rooms he *seems* to be a member of society, though, in fact, the whole universe is the temple in which he displays his devotion to one only God, who, having set nostalgia in his heart, sends him His prophets for comfort at long-spaced intervals.

Though love cannot do without desire, nor hope without satisfaction, it should be noted that neither the one nor the other strictly speaking constitute passion, but only the conditions in which the miracle can take form. They are the two poles between which the spark flashes. Love bursts into flower in the space of time which elapses between the first call of the flesh and the caress which answers it. The narrator's misfortune arises from the fact that an education at once strict and accommodating, combined with a personal tendency to analysis, has caused him to experience at a very early age this especial type of tension. Some children have weak mothers who give in to their every whim. Others, who do not fear the dark, and are therefore unaware of the comfort which another's presence might afford them, go to sleep as soon as they are sent to bed. Marcel is one of those unfortunates on whom nothing ever smiles, or, rather, one of those difficult characters who read portents into all the most ordinary circumstances of life and, with a predisposition to suffering, create, in spite of themselves, occasions for finding it. Deprived of his mother, he sees all hope of clinging to her vanish into a fabulous future. Resentment, jealousy, despair pour headlong in upon him. His need for tenderness becomes diverted, is taken in charge by nerves which vibrate like stretched cords in all his body. His mind, roused to a state of watchfulness, expends much ingenuity on imparting its awareness to the flesh, invents stratagems, foresees complications, and so imprisons the unfortunate young man in a tortuous labyrinth of tactical shifts. Heavily burdened and held in check, desire, with him, is bogged down in a love of which, in actual fact, it is an aberration.

—Georges Piroué, *Proust's Way: An Essay in Descriptive Criticism*, (Melbourne, London, Toronto: William Heinemann Ltd, 1957): 41–44.

Wallace Fowlie on Swann's Dual Experience

[Former Professor Emeritus of French at Duke University, Wallace Fowlie is the author of *Climate of Violence: French Literary Tradition from Baudelaire to the Present*, and *French Literature: Its History and Its Meaning*. He was also a highly prolific translator of French literature, notably the poetry of Rimbaud and Baudelaire. Here he describes Swann's circumstances in terms of the tension between creative and destructive forces or impulses.]

Un Amour de Swann, the second section of *Du Côté de chez Swann*, has been often looked upon as a separate novel that interrupts the life story of the protagonist. In reality, this episode has innumerable bonds with all parts of the work, and the significance of Swann's role becomes more evident the closer we read the novel.

The importance of Charles Swann, at least in the three divisions of *Du Côté de chez Swann*, is clear. In *Combray* he is the refined and rather mysterious friend who visits the boy's parents. We are made aware of his intelligence, his erudition, his elegance of manner and dress. We even learn some things about him that Marcel's family does not know: his cordial relations with the highest society, with the aristocratic Guermantes, even with the Prince of Wales. For the boy Marcel, M. Swann is a gentleman of sympathetic kindness, endowed with great prestige, who stands out as an almost godlike figure in *Combray*. In the second division, *Un Amour de Swann*, Swann is the protagonist and the story is centered on his love for Odette: the origin of his love, the experience of suffering and jealousy, and love's end. In the third division, *Noms de Pays: le Nom*, Swann plays a more effaced, a more subtle role. Marcel's dreams about Balbec and Italy have been somewhat induced by Swann's conversations and allusions. The boy's dreams about Gilberte, and his love for her in the Champs-Elysées scenes, are also dreams about the name of Swann and the strong attraction the boy feels for the glamorous Mme Swann. One always feels behind the sentimental boyish love of Marcel for Gilberte, the stronger, more violent and more deeply analyzed love of Swann for Odette.

Un Amour de Swann is far more than a separate monograph on passion. Swann, as Marcel's precursor, is related to the two "ways"; his own way, first, which leads us to Odette, and the Verdurin clan where Swann sees Odette, and to Elstir (or rather, M. Biche), the painter, and the work of the composer Vinteuil. But Swann is also a close friend of Oriane, duchesse de Guermantes, and of the baron de Charlus, both of whom represent Guermantes' Way. Swann's daughter, Gilberte, will finally marry a Guermantes, Robert de Saint-Loup. With this marriage, at the end of the novel, in Mlle de Saint-Loup, the two ways are joined. Thus, *Un Amour de Swann* is the indirect but indispensable prelude to the great social upheaval which will be described in *Le Temps retrouvé*.

Swann's introduction to Odette presents Proust with the opportunity to describe the Verdurins and their little group. All the details of the opening scenes—the unity of the clan (*le petit noyau*), the only partly disguised dictatorial habits of Mme Verdurin (who calls everyone outside her group *les ennuyeux*), the good music they listen to, the dinners, the expeditions to the country on holidays, the demands of fidelity that are made on new and old members of the clan—form brilliant social satire in its close analysis of an upper bourgeois group, neither quite as elevated as the worldly, aristocratically elegant groups, nor as solidly artistic as the company of intense intellectuals. But this first social world of the Verdurins involves other worlds, with secret and not so secret correspondences with one another. The miracle of Proust's novel is the relationships established between every character, every scene, every theme, within the entire work.

The seemingly isolated episode, *Un Amour de Swann*, is in reality, then, as indispensable as *Combray* is to the meaning of the novel. *Combray* covers childhood when a boy has to submit to the affectionate tyranny of grown-ups, when he is mystified and tormented by the mysterious bonds of affection and sentiment and the painful yearnings of an ill-defined vocation. *Un Amour de Swann* concerns adulthood, when a man is overpowered by the tyrannical suffering of passion, when he is mystified and tormented by the inability to communicate his thoughts or to know the thoughts of the woman he loves, when he is harassed by an incapacity to fulfill his vocation.

Finally the two stories of Combray and Swann's love are resumed in Marcel's obsession with names, with his dreams of Balbec and Venice—two escapes from the beloved but overfamiliar Combray, and with Gilberte, who is a Swann, and therefore distant and unapproachable, who yet draws him dangerously outside of the charmed circle of family, outside the absolutely secure and undoubted love of his mother and grandmother.

Swann is first introduced to Odette de Crécy at the theatre. He has heard of her beauty and knows her reputation as a *demi-mondaine* or *cocotte*. At this first meeting he is indifferent to her special kind of beauty and feels no desire for her. Odette becomes attached to Swann and asks to see his art collection. She introduces Swann to the Verdurins. Against the two backgrounds of the Verdurin salon and Odette's apartment on the rue la Pérouse, with its Chinese art objects and vases of chrysanthemums and cattleyas, her favorite flowers, Swann's mild interest in her grows into a passion and jealous suffering which abates and then completely disappears. At this point Swann marries Odette de Crécy.

At first Swann was amused at her mania for using English words in her conversation, flattered by her attentions and her seeming eagerness to know about the essay he was writing on Vermeer de Delft. Early in their relationship he was struck by Odette's resemblance to Zephora, daughter of Jethro, in a Botticelli fresco of the Sistine Chapel. Swann's sexual relationships were usually with chambermaids or common women but in his relationships with other women (such as Odette or the duchesses he knew), he elevated the relationship to an aesthetic plane. The character of Swann is denigrated only by *muflerie*, a word difficult to translate, which seems to suggest a form of caddishness, a callous insensitivity. On most occasions Swann demonstrates marked delicacy of feeling, but he has his moments of loutishness.

One evening at the Verdurins, while a pianist is playing, Swann hears a phrase from a work for piano and violin he heard the year before, which he very much liked, but which he had not been able to identify. Now, in the Verdurin salon he learns it is the andante movement from Vinteuil's sonata for piano and violin. He asks about Vinteuil's life and work. This musical phrase, described as ethereal and sweet-smelling (*aérienne et odorante*), Swann associates with his love for Odette. With this theme, which will grow in importance throughout the novel, Proust states the problem of the relationship between love and suffering, between happiness and art. It will explain, to some degree, Swann's incomprehensible choice of Odette. The Botticelli painting and the *petite phrase* of Vinteuil's sonata reveal the aesthetic basis of his love for Odette.

Like all love affairs, Swann's love for Odette is composed of rites which have special meanings only for them: the face of Zephora in a painting, a high sustained note in a sonata, the cattleyas which Swann arranges in Odette's corsage and which is the reminder of love-making, since he did this for the first time on the night he possessed her. Swann sacrifices more interesting social relations for the privilege of attending the Verdurins' salon where he can see Odette. The Verdurins will finally turn against him and ostracize him in favor of a new admirer of Odette, a titled gentleman named de Forcheville, but not before he has fallen deeply in love with Odette.

Swann suffers the full impact of his realization of losing Odette, when one evening he does not find her at the Verdurins. He looks for her in the restaurants in Paris where he thinks she might be. Impelled by the full force of suffering (*cette agitation douloureuse*. I, p. 295), he comes to know that his love is now real by the measure of her absence.

Swann's last elaborately narrated encounter with his love occurs at a musical soirée at the marquise de Saint-Euverte's, a lower echelon member of the Guermantes family. Much care is given to the description of Oriane, the princesse des Laumes, the future duchesse de Guermantes. Oriane is not as kind to Mme de Saint-Euverte and to her cousin Mme Gallardon as to her friend Swann. Swann is deeply attached to Oriane, for she reminds him of Combray. (Because of his love for Odette he now has no desire to return to Combray.) That evening Odette recognizes sympathetically Swann's suffering over love. In the midst of these many complex social relationships, Swann hears Vinteuil's sonata being performed, and when the little phrase is played, his suffering becomes so acute that he raises his hand to his heart. Before he can distract his mind all his memories of happiness with Odette overwhelm him: the chrysanthemum petals she threw at him, her handwriting on a letter, the exact line of her eyebrows when once she asked him not to be too long in coming back to her.

For the first time that evening, as he listens to the little phrase of the sonata, Swann feels sympathy and love for Vinteuil, the obscure gifted composer whose work must come from suffering. Vinteuil becomes his partner in suffering, as his little phrase becomes identified with Swann's love for Odette. Vinteuil's music evokes in Swann memories of an entire part of the past just as drinking a cup of tea in tante Léonie's room had for Marcel. The parallel is striking in these first two sections of the novel where Marcel and Swann learn the first great principle Proust the novelist wants to demonstrate: that the soul is not an impenetrable and forbidding void, but the container of a great richness: with explicit reminders for Marcel of happiness, and for Swann of love.

The experience of that evening marks a turning point in Swann's love. He knows then that Odette's love for him, as she once had expressed and felt it, will never return. He resumes his work on Vermeer, while Odette leaves for a visit to Egypt, with Forcheville. Through an anonymous letter, Swann suspects Odette of lesbian relationships, and during their scenes together after her return, he plagues her relentlessly until she confesses. He begins to believe that love is a succession of loves and jealousy a succession of jealousies. His suffering diminishes, and his *muflerie* returns intermittently. The last sentence of *Un Amour de Swann*, one of the most disillusioning statements in the novel, is Swann's claim that he has wasted years of his life and felt his greatest love for a woman whom he did not really love, who was not his type of woman. "*Dire que j'ai gâché des années de ma vie, que j'ai voulu mourir, que j'ai eu mon plus grand amour, pour une femme qui ne me plaisait pas, qui n'était pas mon genre!*" (I, p. 382.)

Swann's liaison with Odette before their marriage is the first full illustration in the novel—prelude to the rest—of the dual experience with which man is involved every moment of life, consciously or unconsciously: the duality of destruction and preservation. Time is the force that slowly and inexorably destroys everything. But memory is time's only deterrent, the one staying factor, the one force for permanence. The scene where by chance Swann hears again Vinteuil's sonata at Mlle de Saint-Euverte's concert is Swann's most exalted moment. At this point in the liaison, he senses that Odette is unfaithful and has become Forcheville's mistress. But before the scene closes, he relives the past: he recaptures what is lost to time. The musical phrase of the sonata, which his sentimentality identified with Odette, forces him, without his willing it, to feel once again the sensations and the gestures and the loving kindnesses that he shared with Odette. These memories are so precisely real as to be almost intolerable. This moment of total recall transcends the mere story of the liaison: its slow beginning, its passion, and its decline.

—Wallace Fowlie, *A Reading of Proust*, (New York: Anchor Books, 1964): 67–72.

RAYMOND T. RIVA ON NAMES

[Raymond T. Riva is Professor Emeritus at the University of Missouri, Kansas City. In this extract, he examines Proust's fascination with names.]

Proust's works are filled with discussions of names: words whose sounds, euphonious or ugly, evoked for him the places or persons themselves. Indeed, one portion of *Du coté de chez Swann* is called "Noms de pays: le nom," and Proust often seems completely preoccupied with names. He definitely felt that names possess a beauty all their own; and throughout his works he used names both to create beauty and to evoke emotion. Thus it is probably not fortuitous that a family name which we learn to dislike is Cambremer (laR, I, 337): this delightfully distasteful word of course evokes an unpleasant image in our minds. But this is only a minor instance. Of far greater significance to our study are those names which evoke in Proust specific images: "Les noms, les noms de pays, les noms de villes, pareils à ces appareils scientifiques qui nous permettent de produire à volonté des phénomènes dont l'apparition dans la nature est rare et irrégulière—nous apportent de la brume, du soleil, des embruns." (Chron, 107.) An example of this is to be found in the following citation, but we must not allow Proust's use of the word "desire" to mislead us. Not only does the author/narrator wish that he could see each of the places mentioned but also he evokes them, creating them out of nothing, in his own mind. His imagination therefore plays a major rôle here, helping visualize places which he has never seen, but whose names are such that he feels he already knows them. (Of course some factual knowledge is prerequisite, otherwise Balbec could not evoke storms at sea nor Florence the lily and Sainte-Marie-des-Fleurs. Yet once this learning process is accomplished, the names may be fully evocative.) "... Balbec, Venise, Florence, dans l'intérieur desquels avait fini par s'accumuler le désir que m'avaient inspiré les lieux qu'ils désignaient. Même au printemps, trouver dans un livre le nom de Balbec suffisait à réveiller en moi le désir des tempêtes et du gothique normand; même par un jour de tempête, le nom de Florence ou de Venise me donnait le désir du soleil, des lys, du palais des Doges et de Sainte-Marie-des-Fleurs." (laR, I, 387.)

It must be admitted that the names of Florence, Venice, and Balbec do contain concrete associations for the boy, and therefore Marcel is able to conjure up images of these places at the sound of their names; yet the sonorities alone of certain names were sufficient to delight him. He would pore over the railroad timetable and take imaginary trips to Balbec, just to have the excuse of pronouncing those wonderful names to himself. We may imagine his delight then when he is to travel on that very train which actually came in contact with these picturesquely named cities and towns (. . .)

There are even more specific ways in which names may be evocative. At the beginning of *A la recherche*, the boy Marcel is using his shadow projector; he throws an image of Golo (itself a wonderful name) onto the wall, and muses about the name of Brabant. Later, he discusses the name of Guermantes: "... impalpables comme l'image de Geneviève de Brabant, ancêtre de la famille de Guermantes, que la lanterne magique promenait sur les rideaux de ma chambre ou faisait monter au plafond,—enfin toujours enveloppés du mystère des temps mérovingiens et baignant, comme dans un coucher de soleil, dans la lumière orangée qui émane de cette syllabe: 'antes.'" (laR, I, 171.) Of course some great part of the charm and delight with these names lies in the fact of their many historical associations: "... je savais qu'ils étaient des personnages réels et actuellement existants, mais chaque fois que je pensais á eux, je me les représentais tantôt en tapisserie, comme était la comtesse de Guermantes dans le 'Couronnement d'Esther' de notre église, tantôt de nuances changeantes, comme était Gilbert le Mauvais dans le vitrail où il passait du vert chou au bleu prune ..." (laR, I, 171.) Thus do the names evoke emotions as well as historical associations. It seems as though the name itself is capable of creating the person, much as the name of Balbec or Florence was capable of creating for the narrator the cities themselves.

Proust's love of aristocratic names for their own sake, as genealogy, need concern us little here. In addition, the discussion of familiar names of aristocratic figures in *A la recherche* (II, 431–433), although of interest to the narrative, has little to interest this study. However, at one time the author shows his attitude toward names themselves. Proust does tell us that in learning the name of a town to have been also a man's name, one adds life to old stones (laR, II, 541). But if the family has no descendants the name will fall out of usage: "... leur nom qu'on n'entend plus jamais, résonne comme un nom inconnu; tout au plus un nom de chose, sous lequel nous ne songeons pas à découvrir le nom d'hommes, survit-il en quelque château, quelque village lointain." (laR, II, 541.) The name Norpois, so long as Marcel thinks it of recent origin, is of little interest to him. But as soon as he learns that a Norpois had existed under Louis XIV, the name takes on the beauty of a carved medallion (laR, II, 540). Thus the historical associations of a name are of great importance to Marcel, the commoner member of aristocratic society. Yet there is far more than mere snobbery in this love for names. Marcel feels a delicious emotion at finding in his historical readings the same name born so haughtily by one of his acquaintances: "... ce prénom même, belle médaille de la Renaissance—d'aucuns disaient un véritable antique—toujours restée dans la famille, ayant glissé de descendant en descendant depuis le cabinet du Vatican jusqu'à l'oncle de mon ami, j'éprouvai le plaisir réservé à ceux qui, ne pouvant faute d'argent constituer un médailler, une pinacothèque, recherchent les vieux noms ..." (laR, I, 749.) Indeed, the very name of the Princess of Parma has so many literary and historical associations that it takes Marcel quite a long time to sift through them all, to be able to reach the person underneath (. . .)

Reality, which he knew, was still overridden by the romantic associations of the name.

Proust's near-intoxication with words and their etymologies literally bursts forth in a lengthy section of *Sodome et Gomorrhe*. The seemingly endless discussion of place names certainly is used to help us analyse Brichot's character, yet Proust himself must have loved them for themselves, or he would not have included so very many (laR, II, 888–892).

Place names so intoxicate Marcel (and therefore really Proust) with their sound that he ascribes to them nonauditory attributes (. . .)

But the very complexity of Proust's feelings for names challenges their description. Names to Proust were an enjoyment and a diversion, and as such cannot be assessed exactly. But we do not feel that be used them merely to overpower the reader, as it might seem, but rather in the hope that the reader should take some of the same pleasure from the interesting, often picturesque names be uses. The name is used less for its own sake than as a means of opening a new, if limited, horizon to us.

—Raymond T. Riva, *Marcel Proust: A Guide to the Main Recurrent Themes*, (New York: Exposition Press, 1965): 195–200

Seth L. Wolitz on the Two Ways

[Gale Professor of Jewish Studies, and Professor of French and Slavic Languages at the University of Texas at Austin, Seth L. Wolitz is the author of *The Hidden Isaac Bashevis Singer*. This is his description of the role played by specific places in Proust's life, and in *Swann's Way*.]

Combray is at the center of Marcel's life. It offers all the possibilities he needs for his development and it is the starting point of his world view. It is clearly a little community, a provincial town. Marcel describes it at first as "no more than a church epitomizing the town.... seen from the railway" (I, p. 37; PI, p. 48) (note the train theme). The church, like the sun moving to either side of the train, or the dancing steeples, symbolizes unity and immortality, the center of life. Combray is self-contained; one knows where it begins and where it ends. Beyond is the unknown: "[the train] would ... proceed across the viaduct, out of the lands of Christendom, of which Combray, to me, represented the farthest limit" (I, p. 98; PI, p. 114). The town consists of a few streets, the names of which echo the medieval origins of the community. The people live in cramped quarters and lead very ordered if not ritualistic lives—Aunt Léonie religiously eats an hour earlier on Saturday (I, p. 84; PI, p. 110), for example, and the townsfolk watch Sunday afternoon maneuvers (I, p. 661: PI, p. 88).

Above all, Aunt Léonie's house, in which Marcel resides, physically represents the starting point of Marcel's Way, which will terminate at the *Matinée*. Different roads lead out of Combray, but only two of them are meaningful to Marcel—Guermantes' Way and Swann's Way. Proust places great emphasis on their differences. "For there were, in the environs of Combray, two 'ways' which we used to take for our walks, and so diametrically opposed that we would actually leave the house by a different door" (I, p. 103; PI, p. 134). One leaves for Swann's Way by the door of Rue St. Esprit (I, p. 104; PI, p. 135) and for Guermantes' Way—which is more difficult to reach—by the garden door of the Rue des Perchamps (I, p. 127; PI, p. 165). The detail underlines the dichotomy in Marcel's mind between the two ways. They are conceived as two separate worlds. "Since my father used always to speak of the 'Méséglise Way' as comprising the finest view of a plain that he knew anywhere, and of the 'Guermantes' Way' as typical of river scenery, I had invested each of them, by conceiving them in this way as two distinct entities, with that cohesion, that unity which belongs only to the figments of the mind" (I, p. 103; PI, p. 134).

Swann's Way offered the road of love, Guermantes' Way was the route to high society. For Swann's Way, the plain is the earth symbol of a contained world of love, as well as a class symbol: the bourgeoisie. The symbol for Guermantes' Way, the river, is that of the aristocracy, of the mystery in life—the poetry of existence, as well as the symbol of a self-contained world. The two ways are the basis of Marcel's emotional and intellectual development. "So the 'Swann's Way' and the 'Guermantes' Way' remain for me linked with many of the little incidents of that one of all the diverse lives along whose parallel lines we are moved, which is the most abundant in sudden reverses of fortune, the richest in episodes; I mean the life of the mind" (I, p. 141; PI, p. 183).

Whereas Marcel meets Swann and knows something about him, the Guermantes are strange poetic demigods. In the name "Guermantes" Proust fuses the title, the persons, and the place name (never seen in *Swann's Way*) into an unreal topography which exists only in Marcel's mind but which contains so much poetry that he will seek to know it in the external world. Georges Poulet, especially, has brought out clearly Marcel's need to synthesize the real and the unknown in order to create the subjective reality and happiness he craves.[8]

The two ways during his youth are distinct. Méséglise, the symbol of unity, is too distant; the great joining must wait many years—for Gilberte and Mlle de Saint-Loup. The "voyage," as I mentioned above, begins at the doorsteps of the home at Combray, at Aunt Léonie's. "And, during the whole of my boyhood, if Méséglise was to me something as inaccessible as the horizon, which remained from sight, however far one went ... Guermantes, on the other hand, meant no more than the ultimate goal, ideal rather than real, of the 'Guermantes Way,' a sort of abstract geographical term .... And so to 'take the Guermantes Way' in order to get to Méséglise, or vice versa, would have seemed to me as nonsensical as proceeding to turn to the east in order to reach the west" (I, p. 103; PI, p. 134).

Thus Marcel sets forth like a Dante with Swann as his guide, sinking into the hell of external life and eventually climbing back to Paradise—the comprehended interior world of the mind.

Note

8. Georges Poulet, "L'Espace Proustien" (Paris: NRF, IIe année, no. 121, 122, 123), III, no. 123, p. 499.

—Seth L. Wolitz, *The Proustian Community*, (New York: New York University Press, 1971): 51-53.

Georges Poulet on Awakening in Space

[Author of such books as *Studies in Human Time*, *The Interior Distance*, and *Who Was Baudelaire?*, Georges Poulet served on the faculties of the University of Edinburgh, Johns Hopkins, and the University of Zurich. This excerpt scrutinizes the opening of *Swann's Way*, in which the narrator, waking in the middle of the night, confusedly struggles to orient himself in space.]

In terms of the title it bears, one knows that the Proustian novel is very exactly a "search for lost time." A being sets out in quest of his past, makes every effort to rediscover his preceding existence. Thus one sees the hero awakening in the middle of the night and asking himself to what epoch of his life there is attached this moment in which he recovers consciousness. This is a moment totally deprived of any connection with the rest of duration, a moment suspended in itself, and profoundly anguished, because the one who lives it does not literally know *when* he lives. Lost in time, he is reduced to an entirely momentary life.

But the ignorance of this awakened sleeper is much graver than it seems. If he does not know *when* he lives, he no longer knows *where* he lives. His ignorance is no less important as to his position in space than as to his position in duration: "And when I awakened in the middle of the night, as I was *ignorant as to where I found myself*, I did not know in the first instant who I was."[1]

The first question that comes to the lips of the Proustian being is, then, no different from that posed at the end by so many of the characters of Marivaux, fallen, as they recognize it willingly, from the moon, and asking themselves in what place and in what moment they find themselves: "I am lost," they say; "my head spins; where am I?" These heedless and charming people do not know where they are; they are all astray, because, in their distraction or their passion, they have lost touch with the world that was theirs. Or, rather—we are on a tragic plane, and in a way of life that hardly resembles Marivaudian heedlessness—the ignorance of the Proustian person is more precisely comparable to the state of mind of that being which Pascal imagines transported, while sleeping, to a desert isle, and awaking there in the morning, in terror, "not knowing where he is, nor the means of getting out."

The being who awakes and who, upon awaking, recovers consciousness of his existence, recovers also consciousness of a span of life singularly and tragically shrunken. Who is he? He no longer knows, and he no longer knows because he has lost the means of relating the place and the moment in which he now lives to all the other places and moments of his former existence. His thought stumbles between times and between places. This moment in which he breathes, is it contiguous to a moment of his infancy, his adolescence, his adulthood? The place where he is, what is it? Is it his bedroom in Combray, or Paris, or one of those hotel rooms, grimmest of all, because, lacking all habitual sympathy with the being who occupies them, they are not real places, they hold nothing personal; they are, so to speak, anywhere in space? On the other hand, for him who awakes in the night, how can he be sure how the place disposes itself? "For an instant," writes Proust in the preface to *Contre Sainte-Beuve*, "I was like those sleepers who on awaking in the night do not know where they find themselves, do not know in what bed, in what house, in what place on earth, in what year of their life they find themselves."[2] Thus, groping, the mind seeks to situate itself. But it has "lost the plan of the place where it finds itself."[3] At random, in the dark, one places the window here, on the opposite side the door; up until the moment when there comes a ray of light, which, making the room clearer, constrains the window to leave its place and to be replaced by the door. So that as chance directs, the order of places rotates and realigns itself from bottom to top. Or as it happened in another episode, in the very same place where the wall of his room rose, the hero, still a child, sees another space appear, a moor on which a horseman rides. But the first space is not abolished; the body of the horseman coincides with the doorknob. Two spaces can then superimpose themselves, the one on the other, as if there were "a wavering and momentary stained window."[4] Now this vacillation, this vertigo, how many times has one not seen it affect the Proustian personage! It comes even when, being fully awake, he is disturbed by an unexpected event. For example, when at the end of an invitation Marcel reads the unhoped-for signature of Gilberte, he cannot believe his eyes; he does not know where he is: "With a vertiginous swiftness this improbable signature played at puss in the corner with my bed, with my chimney, with my wall. *I saw everything waver*, as does someone who falls from a horse."[5]

Wavering of the wall where the child sees Golo astride a horse; wavering of the room where the adolescent receives the first mark of interest from his loved one; wavering, finally, of the room in which the anguished adult awakens in the night. Here are three examples of a dizziness, both interior and exterior, psychical and spatial, which, in three distinct epochs of his existence, affects at one and the same time the mind of the hero and the very places where he finds himself in these three moments. But these moments of vertigo are not the only ones. One remembers the singular episode of the three trees on the way to Hudimesnil. Strange and familiar, never before seen, and yet similar to some image of the past the mind cannot identify again, the paramnesic phenomenon experienced by the mind forbids the thought "to recognize them in the place from which they seemed, so to speak, detached," as well, moreover, to situate them in some other place; so that, adds Proust, "my mind having stumbled between some far off year and the present moment, *the environs of Balbec were wavering ....*"[6]

What wavers here is not only time but place. It is space. A place tries to substitute itself for another place; to take its place. It is the same in an episode even more memorable. At the end of *Le temps retrouvé*, at the house of the Prince of Guermantes, the hero touches his lips with a strongly starched napkin. At once, he says, there surges the dining room at Balbec, "trying to shake the solidity of the House of Guermantes," and "making for an instant all the armchairs waver around me."[7] In a word, just as the bedroom at Combray and the landscape of Golo on horseback, Balbec and the Hotel de Guermantes are vacillating and substitutionable. As do the wall and the moor, they contend for the same place. They are one too many; one usurps the place of the other. The phenomenon of Proustian memory has then not only the effect of making the mind totter between two distinct epochs; it forces it to choose between two mutually incompatible places. The resurrection of the past, says Proust in substance, forces our mind to "oscillate" between years long past and the present time "in the dizziness of an uncertainty like that which one experiences sometimes before an ineffable vision at the moment of going to sleep."[8]

At the moment of going to sleep, at the inverse and corresponding moment of awaking, in the chiaroscuro wherein the consciousness is less prepared to withstand the phenomena that trouble it, the Proustian personage sometimes sees space split up, divided in two, losing its apparent simplicity and immobility. And it can be that this experience should have, for him who experiences it, a vertiginous happiness. But most of the time, the discovery of the unstable character of places inspires in him, completely on the contrary, a feeling of apprehension and even of horror: "Perhaps the immobility of things about us," writes Proust, "is imposed by our certainty that they are themselves and not others, by the immobility of our thought in face of them. The fact remains that each time I awoke thus, my mind agitating itself, in order to find out, without succeeding, where I was, everything was whirling about me, in the dark: things, countries, years."[9]

"Trying to know where I was...." We see clearly then, from the first moment—one could almost say also: from the first *place*—in the account, the work of Proust asserts itself as a search not only for lost time, but also for lost space. The one is like the other, lost in the same manner, in the sense one says he has lost his way and looks for his road. But lost also in the sense one says he has lost his baggage, lost like the beads of a necklace that is broken. How to string together again the place where one is, the moment when one lives, to all the other moments and places that are scattered all along a vast expanse? One could say that space is a sort of undeterminable milieu where places wander in the same fashion that in cosmic space the planets wander. Yet the movement of the planets is calculable. But how does one calculate the movement of places that are wandering? Space does not frame them; it does not assign them one unchangeable position. As happens sometimes in the images of our thought, nothing contests the fact, says Proust, that a piece of landscape brought to the shore of today, "detaches itself so completely from everything, that it floats uncertain in my thought like a flowering Delos, without my being able to say from what country, from what time—perhaps, very simply, from what dream—it comes."[10]

Delight of seeing the image of a place of which we cannot determine the origin move in our mind, like a beautiful ship without a home port. But most often anguish, the anguish of seeing the mobility of places aggravate still more the mobility, already so frightening in itself, of our being. For how is one not to lose his faith in life, when he perceives that the only fixity he believed he found there—a fixity of places, a fixity of objects that are situated there—is illusory? The mobility of places takes away our last shelter. It raises our anchor. To what are we able to cling, if, like times and like beings, places are also swept on in this course that can lead only to death?

Finally, the mobility of places has as a consequence the respective isolation of these places, the ones in relation to the others. If places move about, unless they do so at the same speed and go in the same direction (but alas! we know on the contrary that their courses are essentially aberrant!) forcibly there must change also the apparently constant relationships that linked them to other places and that made of space a network of stable correspondences and proportions. The distance from Paris to Balbec varies; that from Balbec to Raspelière also. In brief, the absence or the reinforcing of habits, the attention or the distraction, the fear or the confidence, or, more simply, the substitution of one mode of locomotion for another, sometimes lengthens and sometimes shortens the roads we travel. But also, now and then, a more serious thing, there is no longer any road; the place where one is leads to no other places; it is like an island, isolated on all sides, incapable of prolonging the network of its vanished communications. A place broken off from the rest of the world, which subsists in itself and of itself, like a besieged citadel; a place situated in absence, as a negation or a lack of access to other places; a place that finally seems absolutely lost in the solitude of space: "Having no more any universe, nor any bedroom, nor body, except threatened by the enemies which were surrounding me, except invaded to the bone by fever, I was alone; I wanted to die."[11]

NOTES

1. *Du côté de chez Swann*, vol. I, p. 5. All references are to the Pléiade edition.
2. *Contre Sainte-Beuve*, p. 56.
3. Ibid., p. 68.
4. *Du côté de chez Swann*, vol. I, p. 9.
5. *A l'ombre des jeunes filles en fleur*, vol. I, p. 500.

6. Ibid., p. 717.
7. *Le temps retrouvé*, vol. III, pp. 874–875.
8. Ibid.
9. *Du côté de chez Swann*, vol. I, p. 6.
10. Ibid., p. 184.
11. *A l'ombre des jeunes filles en fleur*, vol. I, p. 667.

—Georges Poulet, *Proustian Space*, (Baltimore and London: Johns Hopkins University Press, 1977): 7-13.

Vladimir Nabokov on Prose Style in *Swann's Way*

[Author of such celebrated novels as *Lolita* and *Pale Fire*, Vladimir Nabokov was also responsible for introducing undergraduates at Wellesley College, and later at Cornell University, to western literature for nearly two decades. In this lecture, he points out some of the more prominent features of Proust's style.]

Style, I remind you, is the manner of an author, the particular manner that sets him apart from any other author. If I select for you three passages from three different authors whose works you know—if I select them in such a way that nothing in their subject matter affords any clue, and if then you cry out with delightful assurance: "That's Gogol, that's Stevenson, and by golly that's Proust"—you are basing your choice on striking differences in style. The style of Proust contains three especially distinctive elements:

1. A wealth of metaphorical imagery, layer upon layer of comparisons. It is through this prism that we view the beauty of Proust's work. For Proust the term *metaphor* is often used in a loose sense, as a synonym for the hybrid form,** or for comparison in general, because for him the simile constantly grades into the metaphor, and vice versa, with the metaphorical moment predominating.

2. A tendency to fill in and stretch out a sentence to its utmost breadth and length, to cram into the stocking of the sentence a miraculous number of clauses, parenthetic phrases, subordinate

clauses, sub-subordinate clauses. Indeed, in verbal generosity he is a veritable Santa.

3. With older novelists there used to be a very definite distinction between the descriptive passage and the dialogue part: a passage of descriptive matter and then the conversation taking over, and so on. This of course is a method still used today in conventional literature, B-grade and C-grade literature that comes in bottles, and an ungraded literature that comes in pails. But Proust's conversations and his descriptions merge into one another, creating a new unity where flower and leaf and insect belong to one and the same blossoming tree.

"For a long time I used to go to bed early." This opening sentence of the work is the key to the theme, with its center in a sensitive boy's bedroom. The boy tries to sleep. "I could hear the whistling of trains, which, now nearer and now farther off, underscoring the distance like the note of a bird in a forest, unfolded for me in perspective the deserted countryside through which a traveller would be hurrying towards the nearest station: the path that he followed being fixed for ever in his memory by the general excitement due to being in a strange place, to doing unusual things, to the last words of conversation, to farewells exchanged beneath an unfamiliar lamp which echoed still in his ears amid the silence of the night; and to the delightful prospect of being once again home." The whistling of the train underscores the distance like the note of a bird in a wind, an additional simile, an inner comparison, which is a typical Proustian device to add all possible color and force to a picture. Then follows the logical development of the train idea, the description of a traveler and of his sensations. This unfolding of an image is a typical Proustian device. It differs from Gogol's rambling comparisons by its logic and by its poetry. Gogol's comparison is always grotesque, a parody of Homer, and his metaphors are nightmares, whereas Proust's are dreams.

A little later we have the metaphorical creation of a woman in the boy's sleep. "Sometimes, too, just as Eve was created from a rib of Adam, so a woman would come into existence while I was sleeping, conceived from some strain in the position of my thigh.... My body, conscious that its own warmth was permeating hers, would strive to become one with her, and I would awake. The rest of humanity seemed very remote in comparison with this woman whose company I had left but a moment ago: my cheek was still warm with her kiss, my body bent beneath the weight of hers. If, as would sometimes happen, she had the appearance of some woman whom I had known in waking hours, I would abandon myself altogether to the sole quest of her, like people who set out on a journey to see with their own eyes some city that they have always longed to visit, and imagine that they can taste in reality what has charmed their fancy. Gradually, the memory of her would dissolve and vanish, until I had forgotten the daughter of my dream." Again we have the unfolding device: the quest of the woman likened to people who journey to places, and so forth. Incidental quests and visitations and disappointments will form one of the main themes of the whole work.

The unfolding may cover years in a single passage. From the boy dreaming, waking, and failing asleep again, we pass imperceptibly to his habits of sleeping and waking as a man, in the present time of his narration. "When a man is asleep, he has in a circle round him the chain of the hours, the order of years and worlds. Instinctively, when he awakes, he looks to these, and in an instant reads off his own position on the earth's surface and the amount of time that has elapsed during his slumbers.... But for me [as a man] it was enough if, in my own bed, my sleep was so heavy as completely to relax my consciousness; for then I lost all sense of the place in which I had gone to sleep, and when I awoke at midnight, not knowing where I was, I could not be sure at first who I was; I had only the most rudimentary sense of existence, such as may lurk and flicker in the depths of an animal's consciousness; I was more destitute of things than the cave-dweller; but then the memory, not yet of the place in which I was, but of various other places where I had lived, and might now very possibly be, would come like a rope let down from heaven to draw me up out of the abyss of not-being, from which I could never have escaped myself...."

The body's memory would then take over, and "would make an effort to deduce first from the form which its tiredness took the orientation of its various members, and then to deduce from that where the wall lay and the furniture stood, to piece together and to give a name to the house in which it must be living. The body's memory, the composite memory of its ribs, knees, and shoulder-blades, offered it a whole series of rooms in which it had at one time or another slept; while the unseen walls kept changing, adapting themselves to the shape of each successive room that it remembered, whirling through the darkness. And even before my brain, hesitating on the threshold of time and forms, had collected sufficient impressions to enable it to identify the room, it, my body would recall from each room in succession what the bed was like, where the doors were, how daylight came in the windows, whether there was a passage outside, what I had had in my mind when I went to sleep, and had found there when I awoke." We go through a succession of rooms and their metaphors. For a moment he is a child again in a big bed with a canopy, "and at once I would say to myself, 'Why, I must have gone to sleep after all, and Mamma never came to say good night!'" At such a moment he was back in the country with his grandfather, who had died years ago. Then he is at Gilberte's house (she is now Mme. de Saint-Loup) in Swann's old house in Tansonville, and in a succession of rooms in winter and in summer. Finally he actually wakes up in present time (as a man) in his own house in Paris, but his memory having been set in motion: "usually I did not attempt to go to sleep again at once, but used to spend the greater part of the night recalling our life in the old days at Combray with my great-aunt, at Balbec, Paris, Doncières, Venice, and the rest; recalling all the places and people that I had known, what I had actually seen of them, and what others had told me."

Then with this mention of Combray, he is once more in his childhood and back in the time of the narrative: "At Combray, as every afternoon ended, long before the time when I should have to go up to bed, and to lie there, unsleeping, far from my mother and grandmother, my bedroom became the fixed point on which my melancholy and anxious thoughts were centered." When he was especially wretched, the time before dinner was occupied by a magic lantern telling a medieval tale of the evil Golo and the good Geneviève de Brabant (a forerunner of the Duchess de Guermantes). This magic lantern "movement," or "event," becomes connected by the dining-room lamp to the little parlor where the family would adjourn after dinner on wet evenings, and the rain then serves to introduce his grandmother—the most noble and pathetic character in the book—who would insist on walking in the wet garden. Swann is introduced: "we heard, from the far end of the garden, not the profuse and shrill bell which drenched and stunned with its icy, rusty, interminable sound any passing member of the household who set it going by pushing through 'without ringing,' but the double peal—timid, oval, golden—of the visitor's bell.... and then, soon after, my grandfather would say: 'I can hear Swann's voice.' ... Although a far younger man, M. Swann was very much attached to my grandfather, who had been an intimate friend, in his time, of Swann's father, an excellent but an eccentric man in whom the least little thing would, it seemed, often check the flow of his spirits and divert the current of his thoughts." Swann is a man of fashion, an art expert, an exquisite Parisian greatly in vogue in the highest society; but his Combray friends, the narrator's family, have no idea of his position and think of him only as the son of their old friend, the stockbroker. One of the elements of the book is the various ways in which a person is seen by various eyes, as for instance Swann through the prism of Marcel's great aunt's notions: "One day when he had come to see us after dinner in Paris, and had apologized for being in evening clothes, Françoise [the cook], when he had gone, told us that she had got it from his coachman that he had been dining 'with a princess.' 'Some princess of the demi-monde, a courtesan,' drawled my aunt; and she shrugged her shoulders without raising her eyes from her knitting, serenely ironical."

One essential difference exists between the Proustian and the Joycean methods of approaching their characters. Joyce takes a complete and absolute character, God-known, Joyce-known, then breaks it up into fragments and scatters these fragments over the space–time of his book. The good rereader gathers these puzzle pieces and gradually puts them together. On the other hand, Proust contends that a character, a personality, is never known as an absolute but always as a comparative one. He does not chop it up but shows it as it exists through the notions about it of other characters. And he hopes, after having given a series of these prisms and shadows, to combine them into an artistic reality.

The introduction ends with Marcel's description of his despair when visitors forced him to say goodnight downstairs and his mother would not come up to his bedroom for a goodnight kiss; and the story proper begins with a particular arrival of Swann: "We were all in the garden when the double peal of the gate-bell sounded shyly. Everyone knew that it must be Swann, and yet they looked at one another inquiringly and sent my grandmother scouting." The metaphor of the kiss is complex and will run through the whole work. "I never took my eyes off my mother. I knew that when they were at table I should not be permitted to stay there for the whole of dinner-time, and that Mamma, for fear of annoying my father, would not allow me to give her in public the series of kisses that she would have had in my room. And so I promised myself that in the dining-room as they began to eat and drink and as I felt the hour approach, I would put beforehand into this kiss, which was bound to be so brief and stealthy in execution, everything that my own efforts could put into it: would look out very carefully first the exact spot on her cheek where I would imprint it, and would so prepare my thoughts that I might be able, thanks to these mental preliminaries, to consecrate the whole of the minute Mamma would allow me to the sensation of her cheek against my lips, as a painter who can have his subject for short sittings only prepares his palette beforehand, and from what he remembers and from rough notes does in advance everything which he can possibly do in the sitter's absence. But that night, before the dinner-bell had sounded, my grandfather said with unconscious ferocity: 'The little man looks tired; he'ld better go up to bed. Besides, we are dining late tonight.' ...

"I was about to kiss Mamma, but at that moment the dinner-bell rang.

"'No, no, leave your mother alone. You've said good night quite enough. These exhibitions are absurd. Go on upstairs.'"

The agony the young Marcel undergoes, the note he writes to his mother, his anticipation, and his tears when she does not appear foreshadow the theme of despairing jealousy he will endure, so that a direct connection is established between his emotions and Swann's emotions. He imagines that Swann would have laughed heartily could he have seen the contents of the letter to his mother, "whereas, on the contrary, as I was to learn in due course, a similar anguish had been the bane of his life for many years, and no one perhaps could have understood my feelings at that moment so well as himself; to him, that anguish which lies in knowing that the creature one adores is in some place of enjoyment where oneself is not and cannot follow—to him that anguish came through Love, to which it is in a sense predestined, by which it must be taken over and specialized .... And the joy with which I first bound myself apprentice when Françoise returned to tell me that my letter would be delivered, Swann, too, had known well that false joy which a friend can give us, or some relative of the woman we love, when on his arrival at the private house or theatre where she is to be found, for some ball or party or 'first night' at which he is to see her, he finds us wandering outside, desperately awaiting some opportunity of communicating with her. He recognises us, greets us familiarly, and asks what we are doing there. And when we invent a story of having some urgent message to give to her (his relative or friend), he assures us that nothing could be more simple, takes us in at the door, and promises to send her down to us in five minutes .... Alas! Swann had learned by experience that the good intentions of a third party are powerless to control a woman who is annoyed to find herself pursued even into a ball-room by a man whom she does not love. Too often, the kind friend comes down again alone.

"My mother did not appear, but with no attempt to safeguard my self-respect (which depended upon her keeping up the fiction that she had asked me to let her know the result of my search for something or other) made Françoise tell me, in so many words 'There is no answer'—words I have so often, since then, heard the janitors of public dancing-halls and the flunkeys in gambling-clubs and the like, repeat to some poor girl, who replies in bewilderment: 'What! he's said nothing? It's not possible. You did give him my letter, didn't you? Very well, I shall wait a little longer.' And just as she invariably protests that she does not need the extra gas which the janitor offers to light for her, and sits on there ... so, having declined Françoise's offer to make me some tisane or to stay beside me, I let her go off again to the servants' hall, and lay down and shut my eyes, and tried not to hear the voices of my family who were drinking their after-dinner coffee in the garden."

This episode is followed by a description of the moonlight and silence which perfectly illustrates Proust's working of metaphors within metaphors.

The boy opens his window and sits on the foot of his bed, hardly daring to move lest he be heard by those below. (1) "Things outside seemed also fixed in mute expectation." (2) They seemed not to wish "to disturb the moonlight." (3) Now what was the moonlight doing? The moonlight duplicated every object and seemed to push it back owing to the forward extension of a shadow. What kind of a shadow? A shadow that seemed "denser and more concrete than the object" itself. (4) By doing all this the moonlight "made the whole landscape at once leaner and larger like [*additional simile*] a map which is unfolded and spread out" flat. (5) There was some movement: "What had to move—the leafage of some chestnut-tree, for instance—moved. But its punctilious shiver [*what kind of shiver?*] complete, finished to the least shade, to the least delicate detail [*this fastidious shiver*] did not encroach upon the rest of the scene, did not grade into it, remaining clearly limited"—since it happened to be illumined by the moon and all the rest was in shadow. (6) The silence and the distant sounds. Distant sounds behaved in relation to the surface of silence in the same way as the patch of moonlit moving leafage in relation to the velvet of the shade. The most distant sound, coming from "gardens at the far end of the town, could be distinguished with such exact 'finish,' that the impression they gave of remoteness [*an additional simile follows*] seemed due only to their 'pianissimo' execution [*again a simile follows*] like those movements on muted strings" at the Conservatory. Now those muted strings are described: "although one does not lose one single note," they come from "outside, a long way from the concert hall so that [*and now we are in that concert hall*] all the old subscribers, and my grandmother's sisters too, when Swann gave them his seats, used to strain their ears as if [*final simile*] they had caught the distant approach of an army on the march, which had not yet rounded the corner" of the street.

NOTE

** VN illustrates a simple simile as "the mist was like a veil"; a simple metaphor as "there was a veil of mist"; and a hybrid simile as "the veil of the mist was like the sleep of silence," combining both simile and metaphor. Ed.

—Vladimir Nabokov, *Lectures on Literature*, (New York: Harcourt Brace, 1980): 212-215.

J. M. COCKING ON COMBRAY

[J. M. Cocking is one of the most prominent internationally recognized authorities on Proust, and author of *Imagination: A Study in the History of Ideas*. In this discussion of Combray, Cocking identifies the significance of past places for Proust, and describes how Combray emerges from the episode with the madeleine.]

The atmosphere of apocalypse generated by the superb narrative of the *madeleine* incident and the introduction surrounds the whole of the Combray episode. The imperfect tense lifts even specific and apparently singular happenings out of the world of temporal succession; events and scraps of conversation are reported in this tense of habit and extension, of actions and feelings which are never thought of as ending in a recordable achievement; which, as parts of life, are irremediably lost, but, recovered in words, are the significant extensions and dimensions of the past's substance. 'J'avoue', wrote Proust, 'que certain emploi de l'imparfait de l'indicatif—de ce temps cruel qui nous présente la vie comme quelque chose d'éphémère à la fois et de passif, qui, au moment même où il retrace nos actions, les frappe d'illusion, les anéantit dans le passé sans nous laisser comme le parfait, la consolation de l'activité—est resté pour moi une source inépuisable de mystérieuses tristesses."[55] Many events are thrust back into the pluperfect; seen, that is, not as part of the succession of a moving life but as subsisting only in their effects, in their lasting contribution to the tensions and assumptions which are part of Marcel's background.

The anguish of bedtime is the first sign of the serpent in Marcel's Eden, the first instance of the way in which events refuse to adapt themselves to wishes. There are other foreshadowings of a future to be lived in a fallen world. Yet Combray is stability and security, with its limitations offset by the freedom of a vivid and lively imagination nourished on books, and not yet aware that its failure to be self-sufficient promises disillusion. At this stage we are given the delight in the illusions themselves, the promises later to be betrayed.

Stability, security, tradition, habit, all these are summed up in the church solidly and comfortably ensconced in time, a visible and permanent past. The church is the first part of Combray to be seen, after Marcel's bedroom, and if we leave it to meet Aunt Léonie drinking her lime-flower tea we soon return to explore its detail. For it is a symbol of what the novel sets out to be; in *Le Temps retrouvé*, at the very end of the book, we are told that Marcel's great work is to have 'la forme que j'avais pressentie autrefois dans l'église de Combray, et qui nous reste habituellement invisible, celle du Temps'.[56] For Proust the only essence is that of destiny completed, the only contemplation of essence is the contemplation of the essence of a completed past. In *Le Temps retrouvé* his white-haired and wrinkled characters have achieved a kind of grandeur by achieving a past, their only real dimension. Combray church and Balbec church, symbols of Amiens and all the mediaeval churches to the significance of whose iconography Proust had been awakened by Ruskin and Mâle, are, like Proust's novel, means of renewing in contemplation a lost spiritual vigour.

The past is solidity; it is also romance. Every symbol of the past is a window for the imagination on to the glamour of legend. The ancient porch of the church gives access not only to the finger-worn holy water stoup, the tomb covering the noble dust of the abbots of Combray and the peacock colours of the windows, but, by suggestion, to a grotto hung with stalactites, a valley visited by fairies and the mystery of a Merovingian darkness. Stimulating to the imagination, yet static, familiar and unthreatening; offering the rich essence of time with none of time's menace of change, the church has the degree of its past extension marked in the varieties of its architecture and ornament, reflecting the preoccupations, tastes and spiritual qualities of many periods. And its steeple is the symbol of a world clear of Proust's oppressive sense of guilt, the centre of the *vertus de Combray*; they, the steeple and Marcel's grandmother are grouped together in Marcel's memory.

It is the privilege of childhood to combine routine and freedom, security and imaginative adventure; Marcel is so morbidly dependent on the familiar that he is a little afraid even of the freedom and adventure of imagination. The magic lantern which covers the walls of the bedroom where he suffers the prospect of the nightly separation from his mother with coloured pictures of Geneviève de Brabant's castle and Golo on horseback 'filled with dreadful purpose' is an intimation of supernatural mystery and beauty, but also an uncomfortable intrusion into the world of comfortable habit. There are, in the last event, only two ways in which Marcel can adjust imagination and reality; by dulling imagination through habit, or by escaping from reality into books. Habit is the drug which deadens the pain experienced by the imaginative self in a hostile reality.

But imagination is not to be denied; and between habit and art there lie the alternately ecstatic and dispiriting rhythms of illusion and disillusion. In the Combray episode, almost the whole of the child's world is caught up on the tide of poetry, as the doorknob and all the natural irregularities in the walls of Marcel's room are caught up out of their material function by the light of the magic lantern and absorbed into the 'supernatural essence' of Golo and his horse; this complex of the sensuous pleasure of colour, historical exoticism and the emotions connected with Golo's vaguely ominous descent on Geneviève's castle is one of the determinants of Marcel's imaginative life; it connects directly and in all its elements with the suggestiveness of the stained glass windows in the church, and the double complex is the source of the poetry which marks the beginning of what Marcel, using one of Bergson's terms, calls the '*durée*' of the name Guermantes in his own mind—for Oriane de Guermantes is a descendant of the historical Geneviève. Elements drawn from his later imagining as stimulated by books gravitate towards and crystallize round this double nucleus; and before this particular poetic world is thrown off its orbit by the first sight of Oriane in the flesh, he is already more than half in love with her as he has created her for himself.

NOTES

55. CSB, p. 170.
56. ARTP III, p. 1045.

—J. M. Cocking, *Proust: Collected Essays on the Writer and His Art*, (Cambridge: Cambridge University Press, 1982): 53-55.

PHILIP THODY ON THE GOOD-NIGHT KISS

[Former Professor Emeritus of French at the University of Leeds, Philip Thody wrote extensively on French literature, with particular attention to the Existentialists, Genet, and Barthes. His books include *Albert Camus: A Study of His Work*, *Jean-Paul Sartre: A Literary and Political Study*, and *The Conservative Imagination: From Edmund Burke to Tom Stoppard*. In this passage, he subjects the good-night kiss, and the relationship it reveals between Marcel and his mother, to a Freudian reading.]

The author who writes in *Du côté de chez Swann* about 'the vast unfathomed and forbidding night of the soul which we take to be an impenetrable void',[58] also seems to have hit upon a very important Freudian concept, even if he has never read a word by Freud himself. This impression is even stronger if you look at what happens in the novel.

Thus at the very beginning of *Du côté de chez Swann*, even

before the experience of the 'petite madeleine' and the section subtitled *Combray*, there is the episode known as 'le drame du coucher' (the drama of the good-night kiss). It is this which has the strongest Freudian overtones, and which led a reviewer in *The Times Literary Supplement* on 12 December 1940 to make the very accurate comment that Proust himself was 'superlatively well acquainted with the agonies of the mother fixation'. For every evening, when he is about to go to bed, the Narrator Marcel is heartbroken at the thought that he is going to be separated from his mother. His sole consolation is that she will come upstairs to kiss him goodnight before he finally goes to sleep, but this final kiss never lasts long enough. He would like to call her back and make her kiss him again, but is restrained by the fear of annoying her. This, he knows, will destroy the peace which her good-night kiss has bestowed upon him, and the insistence is on the calm provided by this reassurance of his mother's love rather than on any erotic overtones. But it is not hard to see how the incident could also be interpreted in Freudian terms. The male child, according to Freud's interpretation of the legend in which Oedipus killed his father and married his mother, wants to possess the mother sexually. Proust's explanation in terms of emotional reassurance strikes the thorough-going Freudian as either a wilful or an unconscious refusal to face the facts. Add the knowledge that Proust was also a homosexual, and the hunt is really on. Homosexuals, as any Freudian will tell you, prefer men because they see every woman as a reincarnation of their mother. Because they were taught in their childhood that they could not have her, they are put off women for life.

This Freudian reading becomes less convincing when the 'drame du coucher' is replaced in the context of the novel. For there is, to start with, no hint of any hostility between the Narrator and his father. The jealousy which later becomes so dominant a theme in the whole of *A la recherche du temps perdu* is completely different from the rivalry which Freudians see as existing between fathers and sons, and there is also the question of the Narrator's age. Although Proust's reluctance to mention dates or give his characters a precise age prevents us from telling how old the Narrator is, the general impression is that he is between five and seven. He is old enough to write a letter, though not yet to have read what he calls 'real novels'. He is therefore well past the age of three or four which Freudians see as critical in the development of the Oedipus complex.

Proust would certainly not have been able to write about Marcel's relationship with his mother in the way that he did if he had read Freud. His knowledge of Freudian doctrine would inevitably have coloured his presentation of a drama which has so many apparently obvious Freudian overtones. Either he would have strengthened these to emphasise the similarities; or he would have toned them down to bring out the differences. There is no evidence that he did this, and Proust's account of the causes and the consequences of 'le drame du coucher' has a very different set of implications from those which stem from a Freudian reading. They represent an attitude which is comparable to that of Freud in the importance which it gives to the impact of childhood traumas on the emotional behaviour of adults. But these implications differ very sharply from those of Freud in that everything which happens takes place on the level of the conscious and not of the unconscious mind.

Thus the Narrator in *Du côté de chez Swann* knows exactly why his mother is behaving as she does. Together with her own mother, to whom she is deeply attached, she is trying to make her son a little more emotionally independent. She is trying to cure him of what both she and his father think of as rather silly, unmanly conduct. The Narrator understands and appreciates these motives, and would like to make his mother and grandmother happier by co-operating. But he cannot bring himself to do this—he is, after all, only a child—and is as conscious as they are of his lack of will-power. In this, as in other respects, there is a strong similarity between the Marcel of *A la recherche du temps perdu* and Marcel Proust himself. This is well brought out by George Painter in his biography of Proust, especially in his treatment of the conviction which both Proust and his Narrator had of being lacking in will-power. Nobody, as Painter observed, could have struggled against illness to complete a work as long and complex as *A la recherche du temps perdu* without being quite exceptionally determined, and both Proust and his Narrator are doing themselves less than justice. But Proust did see himself as a weak-willed person and there is ample evidence that the details of 'le drame du coucher' are based upon an incident or a series of incidents in his own life. The episode is described in comparable detail in *Jean Santeuil*, and Marcel's complete emotional dependence on his mother in *Du côté de chez Swann* is matched by Proust's feelings for his mother. When, at the age of thirteen or fourteen, he was asked to define his idea of misery, he replied that it was to be 'séparé de Maman' (separated from Mamma).[59]

The contribution of 'le drame du coucher' to the dominant themes and overall structure of *A la recherche du temps perdu* is nevertheless in no way dependent on the links it had with Proust's own experience. For it is on one of the evenings that Charles Swann comes to dine at Marcel's grandparents' house in Combray that the crisis occurs which the Narrator sees as determining his whole future emotional development, and *Du côté de chez Swann* is carefully constructed, as a work of art, to drive home an immediate dramatic and ironic parallel. Just as the Narrator cannot do without the constant reassurance of his mother's love, so Swann becomes increasingly dependent on the presence of Odette. Just as Marcel is intrigued by what he sees as the mysterious pleasures which his mother is about to enjoy with the other adults at dinner, so Swann becomes obsessed by the sensual delights which he suspects Odette of enjoying not only with other men but also with other women. The episode entitled *Un Amour de Swann* comes so soon after 'le drame du coucher' that there is no way in which the reader can avoid seeing this parallel. In both cases, the writing shows Proust at his most dramatic and effective. The reader can no more fail to identify with the small boy than he can prevent himself from sympathising with the grown man. The irony, of which the Narrator also intends the reader to be fully conscious, is that it is Charles Swann, the one person most able to understand the anguish of 'le drame du coucher', who is responsible for triggering it off.

58. I 350; 382.

59. *CSB* 335–6. The 966 pages of the 1971 Pléiade edition of *Contre Sainte-Beuve* provide a good deal of information about Proust as a man and a literary thinker, not all of which is reproduced in the 201 pages of translation by Sylvia Townsend Warner, published by the Hogarth Press in 1958 and reissued in paperback in 1984. We learn that the fault which he felt most inclined to forgive, at the age of thirteen or fourteen, was the private life of men of genius; that, in his twenties, his favourite literary hero was Hamlet; that the military event he most admired was his own enlistment; his chief defect a lack of will-power; and his greatest need 'to be loved, or, rather, to be more accurate, to be caressed and spoilt, far more than the need to be admired'.

—Philip Thody, *Marcel Proust*, (New York: St. Martin's Press, 1988): 36-39.

PLOT SUMMARY OF

Cities of the Plain

At the end of *The Guermantes Way*, Marcel, now a young man, goes to see the Duc and Duchesse de Guermantes, with whom he has become familiar, to verify an invitation he has received from the Princesse de Guermantes. During this visit to the Hôtel de Guermantes (a large subdivided building containing both living quarters and places of business), Marcel witnesses an event the account of which he postpones to the beginning of *Cities of the Plain*. Waiting to see the Guermantes, he, from hiding, witnesses a rather grotesque flirtation between the Baron de Charlus, coming to visit an elderly relative, and the former tailor Jupien, who has a shop in the Hôtel. Marcel suddenly realizes that Charlus is a homosexual, and that his strange behavior towards Marcel was actually a form of flirtation. Being exceedingly curious, Marcel follows Charlus into Jupien's shop unobserved, and overhears their intercourse in the office. This provides Marcel an occasion to reflect at length on homosexuality itself, the "race upon which a curse is laid," descended from the people of Sodom and Gomorrah (male and female, respectively), known in the Bible as the Cities of the Plain. He describes the loneliness, the secrecy, the fear and shame, the hasty and secretive consummations, associated with homosexual desire. Marcel's discovery of Charlus' homosexuality not only causes Charlus' character to become considerably clearer, it brings out into the open a theme which had up until this point been submerged in the broader narrative, and which will henceforth be one of the leitmotifs of *In Search of Lost Time*. And, for all the secrecy and shame associated with homosexuality, it will prove to be a trait shared by a great many of the novel's characters.

There follows a lengthy description of the Princesse de Guermantes' reception. The Prince and Princesse de Guermantes occupy the highest possible position in Parisian society, and Marcel spends much of the evening angling for an introduction to the Prince. Shortly after this introduction is finally effected, Marcel observes the Prince speaking privately in the garden with Swann. During this conversation, Swann reveals to the Prince that he is dying of cancer. The Duc and Duchesse de Guermantes are present as well, the Duchesse at one point snubbing Odette and Gilberte, who have come with Swann. There is much discussion of the Dreyfus case, and a wide variety of points of view are expressed on the case, although the general tendency seems to be swinging gradually to the Dreyfusard side. Charlus is in rare form, and is playing up his false reputation as a womanizer. Marcel's young friend Robert de Saint-Loup, a member of the Guermantes family whom he met in *Within A Budding Grove*, arrives and also makes ostentatious displays of his heterosexuality (his affairs with men will be revealed in later volumes). The reader is also surprised to discover that the Princesse de Guermantes, a famous beauty and easily the most desired woman in Paris, is secretly infatuated with Charlus.

Shortly after the evening of the party, Albertine contacts Marcel. He began a flirtation with her in *Within A Budding Grove*, an affair which advanced somewhat in *The Guermantes Way*, and somewhat further here. After she leaves, he is able to write to Gilberte without the slightest emotion. Marcel receives word that, as Swann himself is declining and dying, Odette's own salon, centered around Bergotte, is flourishing.

The next section is granted the title Proust had originally chosen for the entire novel, "The Intermittencies of the Heart," referring to the strange inconstancy of human emotions, the way in which a feeling comes and goes in accord with unconscious cues. Marcel returns to Balbec, having become sexually interested in a servant employed by one of the Duchesse de Guermantes' aristocratic friends currently staying there. Disappointed in this ambition, Marcel succumbs to a growing sense of utter emptiness. Then, while untying his shoes in his hotel room, he is suffused with a miraculous sense of the presence of his grandmother, who died in *The Guermantes Way*. It is like those scenes of involuntary memory invoked elsewhere, in which a random cue triggers a powerful emotional response; in this case, Marcel at once feels saved and returned to himself by the abrupt presentiment of his grandmother's living presence, and also deeply aggrieved, because this effect is possible only across the distance separating them. With bleak clarity, Marcel realizes he has lost his grandmother forever.

In his grief, Marcel withdraws momentarily from those around him. He continues to see his mother, and notices how strongly she has come to resemble his grandmother, as though death had brought mother and daughter closer together as well. Toward the end of this period, Marcel is seized with a sudden desire to see Albertine again.

At his request, Albertine joins Marcel in Balbec. Their love affair blooms, but he is jealous, and suspicious of her. He has not forgotten the example set by Odette, and begins to notice Albertine's evasions and misrepresentations. They visit a casino, and Marcel notices Albertine staring with apparent appetite at someone reflected in a large mirror—two young women, rumored to be lovers. Marcel has learned two things from the story of Swann and Odette: that jealousy is the strongest emotion at work in keeping people together, and that this depends on giving the impression of unreturned love. So, in order to keep Albertine, Marcel treats her coolly, and pretends to care more for her friend Andrée. At one point, Marcel confronts Albertine, asking if she and Andrée have ever been more than friends; Albertine denies it, but this is a lie.

A scandal erupts at Marcel's hotel involving the two young ladies from the casino, one of whom is Bloch's sister.

Marcel and Albertine go to Donciére to visit Saint-Loup, and, while waiting on the station platform, witness the first meeting between the Baron de Charlus and the handsome young violinist, Charles Morel. Later, at a soirée hosted by the Verdurins, Charlus and Morel arrive together. It is clear that, however misjudged he may be by Parisian aristocratic society, the bourgeois Verdurins and their circle, who are themselves pretenders of another sort, have no illusions about Charlus' homosexuality. In person, Morel is an effeminate, arrogant, erratic youth, socially chaotic but an immensely gifted musician. He is plainly not one to be cowed into passivity even by Charlus' overbearing personality, nor does his self-centered personality seem capable of returning another's love. At this get-together,

Charlus will have his first restrained confrontation with Mme Verdurin; this conflict inaugurates a protracted period of Charlus' alienation which will come to a head in *The Fugitive*.

Marcel's affair with Albertine reaches its heights; they are constantly together. Sating himself over this period, Marcel gradually begins to tire of Albertine; again, only his jealousy, his need to know what she does during the long hours they spend apart, sustains his interest. Morel's relationship with Charlus becomes increasingly parasitic; Charlus is oblivious to Morel's many infidelities, and has been supplying Morel with money. When, at one point, Morel rebuffs him, Charlus enlists Marcel's help in delivering a letter informing Morel of Charlus' intention to fight a duel. Morel persuades Charlus to call it off, and Charlus is placated, convinced that Morel cares about him. In fact, Morel has been frequenting a high-class brothel in Maineville, where he has dallied with the Prince de Guermantes himself, among others.

Increasingly uncertain about Morel's affections, Charlus cultivates an unlikely interest in Bloch. Marcel, at this time, is seriously reviewing his feelings for Albertine; her aunt badly wants her to marry, but Marcel concludes that a marriage to Albertine would be "madness." He decides to break it off. In casual conversation, Albertine reveals that she is very close to Mlle Vinteuil's female lover. This news stirs Marcel's need for her once again, and far from breaking with her, he begs her to return with him to Paris. She refuses at first, then changes her mind. Once back at home, Marcel discusses the possibility of marriage with his mother, who doesn't approve of his affair. *Cities of the Plain* ends with Marcel's declaration: "I absolutely must marry Albertine."

LIST OF CHARACTERS IN

Cities of the Plain

"Marcel" the anonymous narrator. In this volume, he is a young man, trying to apply the lessons derived from his attention to Swann's love affair to his own relationship with Albertine.

Marcel's mother is uncertain of Albertine, and would rather Marcel end his involvement with her. As she ages, she is becoming more like her own mother: unobtrusively altruistic, unselfish, and ignored.

Marcel's grandmother dies in *The Guermantes Way*. Her presence will be momentarily restored to Marcel in an epiphanic moment, in which he realizes she is gone forever.

Françoise is the family's insensitive servant. She also dislikes Albertine.

The **Baron de Charlus**, whose vanity and arrogance are counterbalanced by the pain and shame associated with his homosexuality, and the abuse he receives from the cold-hearted Morel.

The **Duc de Guermantes** softens somewhat in this volume, shifting his allegiance toward the Dreyfusard party along with most of the rest of the Guermantes.

The **Duchesse de Guermantes** is principally showcased at the party thrown by the Prince and Princesse, in which she exhibits her wicked wit, her uncanny knack for impersonations, her snobbery, and her refusal to know either Odette or Gilberte Swann.

Charles Morel, the mercurial, ill-tempered violinist and object of the Baron de Charlus' affections. He is cold, calculating, and utterly selfish, unfaithful to the Baron and grasping after his money.

Monsieur Verdurin mainly assists his wife in supervising social gatherings. Tormenting the helpless Saniette, a man invited only to serve as the butt of jokes, is his primary recreation.

Madame Verdurin the bourgeois hostess, beginning to take umbrage at Charlus' cavalier treatment of her wishes, and his commandeering of her little circle. Later she will break Morel and Charlus apart and expel Charlus from the group.

Charles Swann, a slowly-fading luminary, is now mortally ill. He retains enough vitality, however, to ogle a generously-shaped woman at the Guermantes reception, and to persuade the Prince de Guermantes to support the Dreyfusard party.

Odette Swann ascends in fame as her husband declines. Now operating a salon in her own right, and succeeding largely due to the influence of Swann's old friend, Bergotte.

Prince de Guermantes a somewhat effete, but loftily masterful man. Like many other characters, he is secretly conducting homosexual affairs, even with Morel.

Princesse de Guermantes is the brightest light in Parisian society, a woman of celebrated beauty and exquisite taste. She harbors a completely hopeless love for Charlus.

Albertine is a beautiful, dark-haired girl, who conceals a strong attraction to other girls. She is the love of Marcel's life, a witty, intelligent, increasingly well-cultivated young woman, addicted to white lies and clandestine meetings.

Andrée, another of the pretty young girls of Balbec, Albertine's wry friend, with whom she occasionally dallies. Marcel routinely feigns interest in her, to make Albertine jealous.

Jupien, a former tailor with a shop in the Hôtel de Guermantes, and Charlus' sometime lover. He facilitates Charlus' relationship with Morel, and puts forward Morel's plan to marry his niece.

Robert de Saint-Loup a Guermantes and one of Marcel's boyhood friends from Balbec. An affable young man who conceals his interest in men behind a slightly over-emphatic gallantry to women.

CRITICAL VIEWS OF
Cities of the Plain

LÉON PIERRE-QUINT ON PROUST'S OBJECTIVE TREATMENT OF HOMOSEXUALITY

[Best known for his biography of Gide, Léon Pierre-Quint is one of the better-known French critics of the twentieth century. One of the earlier commentators on Proust's writings, he notes the unsqueamish manner in which Proust deals with "inversion" or male homosexuality.]

"That [which the sexual inverts] call their love (and, to which, out of a social sense, playing on the word, they have annexed all that poetry, painting, music, chivalry, and asceticism have been able to add to love) flows, not from an ideal of beauty which they have chosen, but from an incurable *malady*." This quotation contains practically the whole of Marcel Proust's thoughts upon this vexatious problem.

For Marcel Proust inversion is a pathological fact which from this point of view concerns principally, and even solely, physicians and psychiatrists: a pathological, physiological, and neurological fact, which in no way affects the general psychology of the individual. The invert's passion is the same as that of the normal man, in the sense that it dashes itself, like every other amorous passion, against the rocks of anxiety and jealousy, that it is submitted to the tormenting force of crystallization, that it is familiar with eternal vows that acknowledge no to-morrow, with the yielding up of self to the point of sacrifice, the bewilderment and ephemerality of all the movements of the conscience. But the invert, more luckless than mankind in general, and set under a curse by society, is obliged to defend himself against it, to conceal his dearest, his deepest, his most moving aspirations, and to struggle in hypocrisy, far more than other men, to achieve his happiness. Marcel Proust, in his perpetual searching of the pleasures of life, encountered a certain group of hapless individuals. What brought him to measure the impression they left on him was that he felt in them, under a form at once exacerbated and highly intensified, the desire to find whole-hearted joy: that he felt their fettered impulses, that he felt, chief of all, their love. He saw in them the age-old struggle of the individual against society. Apart from the obstacles which a man finds within himself, when he wants to affirm himself, to seek his own happiness—such as his incapacity to come out of himself, to hold and fix an emotion of happiness—we find society adding all kinds of hindrances. And these overwhelm the invert more especially. Proust thus comes to regard him as the symbolic victim of society. This conception of sexual inversion is at all points in direct opposition to that of the writers who have made allusion to the topic.

Many poets, no doubt, heedless of reality and letting their voices sing within themselves, have been unable to resign themselves to the belief that a passion which gave birth to sentiments of tenderness as pure and disinterested as those of Romeo or of des Grieux found its origins in an involuntary malady of the brain. These poets, imagining that they were studying inversion, have actually only been speaking of neighbouring and kindred passions, which are capable of being confounded with it and being substituted for it in their minds and in literature. Some, concealing their subject under the cloak of symbols, evoke only a heavy and troubled atmosphere. They make allusion to debauches, which they wrap about with the perilous veil of beauty. And they are haunted, these writers, by vice, a sumptuous vice, a magnificent nightmare, the fruit of the tree of good and evil, which serves to enrich the monotony of life. Immorality in their eyes is one of the essential motives of art. Others, again, seek to idealize it through aesthetics and through ethics. They celebrate friendship, the affection of the master-protector for his disciple, the strength of the masculine body in the gymnasium or beneath the portico, the marvellous characteristics of the adolescent, who is at once the ultimate beauty and the ultimate good.

They draw analogies with antiquity. But in those times all forms of love which had not the continuance of the race as their object were placed on one and the same level, stripped of the mystical, moral, and practical complications which Christianity and our business-like civilization have incorporated with love. For love then was a simple and natural gesture, and in that different state of opinion the idealization of Sodom could be understood. But "for nineteen hundred years now ... all the customary homosexuality of the youths of Plato and the shepherds of Virgil has vanished. There survives only an involuntary homosexuality, that which is concealed from others and travestied even by its representatives." To celebrate inversion as a passion chosen by man of his own free will, from a taste for beauty, friendship, or the masculine intelligence, is an absurdity. Only a few men of genius, great enough and frank-minded enough to live above their own times, in a younger and fresher world, can rise to a superhuman and sublime friendship. The others confound their "mania" with friendship, which, says Proust, "has not the slightest resemblance to it."

Thus it is clear that this passion could not be the expression either of an ideal of beauty, or of an ideal of satanic debauchery: that would imply that it was an act of volition. It is a malady with social consequences. The writer does not naïvely try to raise this passion above its proper level. He observed his characters. He sees nervous "involuntaries" set in the midst of a society which carries a scourge for them. And he adds: "For the invert, vice begins, not when he engages in relations (for too many reasons can command them), but when he takes his pleasure with women." And Proust tells us that "some of them, if one surprises them still in bed in the morning, display an admirable woman's head, so much is the expression general and so much does it symbolize the whole sex." Here the writer, penetrating into one of the most troubling mysteries of nature, sets out several questions, though not answering them; they are questions which are doubtless familiar, but their terms are so perfectly thrown into the light by him that, under his pen, they take on an aspect of tragedy which shakes the firm stance of reason. He is astonished at the way in which, among the men-women, the sexual instinct leads by such certain paths towards a sex opposed to their own—that is to say, towards other men—and triumphs over the aberrations which might drag reason and the social constraints headlong away. "One has but to look at this curly head of hair on the white pillow to understand that if, in the evening, this youth slips from between his parents' fingers, in spite of them, in spite of himself, it will not be to go and find women...."

Proust is thus brought to comparing this passion with certain forms of madness. During a whole conversation the madman in our presence may easily appear to be quite normal, and it is just at the moment of parting that, all of a sudden, he will reveal his madness to us. Similarly, the inverts are just like other men—until the moment when the veil suddenly falls from their fatal love. At the Prince de Guermantes' reception, the author takes a cross-section of the drawing-room: in the remotest corner of the room Charlus, in the middle of a group of his friends, is freely exchanging with them, in their esoteric language, remarks about the manservants and footmen of the hotels or clubs that they frequent.

—Another problem: whence comes it that an insignificant physiological flaw, like an invisible bump on the skull, takes outward manifestation in gestures, in laughter, so effeminate that they seem nothing short of the signs of a madness? How is it that this beginning of hermaphroditism, limited to the development of the haunches and the whiteness of the skin, is often, among the persons affected by it, the mark of a pronounced taste for the arts? A taste, it is true, supported on the false literary idealism that we have explained, but one capable in spite of everything of producing astonishing works.

Certain moral or philosophic theories, no doubt, attempt explanations of this mystery of physiology. In the *Symposium* Plato speaks of "androgynes." Schopenhauer thinks that inversion is a provision of nature in order to sterilize unions in which the old man or the extreme youth, if they were to procreate, would no longer be in the full enjoyment of their faculties.

Marcel Proust adopts none of these general theories. Just as when he declares that he knows nothing which can make him believe in the immortality of the soul, and alludes nevertheless to the possibility of an anterior life, so, in remaining in a state of expectancy, inversion, he thinks, may perhaps be attached to "another and higher law ... to epochs of experimentation, this initial hermaphroditism," an ultimate reversion which would to-day hold in check the excessive forces of fecundity on our over-peopled earth. However, he does not develop this hypothesis. It does not belong to literature, but to the psychiatrists, and these in any case are content to classify and label the maladies.

—Léon Pierre-Quint, *Marcel Proust: His Life and Work*, (New York: Alfred A. Knopf, 1927): 195-200.

FREDERICK CHARLES GREEN ON THE DELAYED IMPACT OF THE DEATH OF MARCEL'S GRANDMOTHER

[Here Green discusses the scene in which Marcel abruptly realizes the fact of his grandmother's death.]

Once again we are reminded that *A la recherche du temps perdu* is not just the story of Marcel's (or Proust's) progressive efforts to understand and interpret the behaviour and the psychological states of the characters whose lives at every moment impinge upon and intermingle with his own life. It is not merely the narrative of his attempts to endow with the beauty or unity of art, to externalize for us, his sensations or impressions of the material world surrounding him. It is also the story of Marcel's gradual discovery that the self, the *moi* called Marcel which is always striving to penetrate by sympathy and at the same time to perceive by the intellect, the reality of external things and people—that this self is never static, never, as Proust says, 'une âme totale', in the sense that all its powers of imagination, sensation, perception and memory are completely and ever available. Sometimes this discovery, as in the present instance, is accompanied by the greatest anguish. Yet does not Proust tacitly imply that this suffering, for the artist, will eventually be tempered by the sense of spiritual satisfaction which comes from the possession of a truth, from the discovery of a reality?

In these pages, I think for the first time, a French novelist expresses in language of surprising lucidity, the reality of a spiritual experience which, although universal, has probably never been so arrestingly externalized by a novelist. Marcel, describes what happens when an everyday action—that of stooping to unbutton his shoes—releases from the subconscious the self, the spiritual state which was his on that evening of his first visit to Balbec. The psychological atmosphere surrounding the original action, like Marcel's image of his grandmother as she really was, had, in the meantime, remained in the Aladdin's cave of the subconscious waiting for the Open Sesame; the repetition of the original action in a milieu and in circumstances re-creating the cadre or ambience of his state of soul at Balbec, of the *moi* which was then Marcel. But why does he only now experience the living reality of his grandmother's death, so long after the fact? Proust explains what he calls this anachronism, this 'lack of synchronization between the calendar of facts and that of our feelings'. True, Marcel had often thought of his grandmother and in the year after her death, had often spoken of her. But other impressions, other memories, the habit of seeing her during her last illness had suppressed the memory of what she had *really* meant to him. 'Car aux troubles de la mémoire sont liées les intermittences du coeur.' Probably, thinks Marcel, it is because of the existence of our body that we are apt to believe that all our past joys and griefs are perpetually in our possession enclosed as in a vase. In point of fact, only a part, often the part least important for our true or spiritual existence, is present in our consciousness. The sensations and emotions that are most truly and profoundly our *moi* are thrust down into that *domaine inconnu*, the subconscious.

> 'Le moi [says Marcel] que j'étais alors et qui avait disparu si longtemps, était de nouveau si près de moi qu'il me semblait encore entendre les paroles qui avaient immédiatement précédé et qui n'étaient pourtant plus qu'un songe, comme un homme mal éveillé croit percevoir tout prés de lui les bruits de son rêve qui s'enfuit.'[1]

This theme, admirably described as 'l'incompréhensible contradiction du souvenir et du néant', has inspired some of the finest pages in world literature. Explored anew by Proust, it acquires a fresh density of meaning, chiefly, no doubt, because

Marcel exfoliates not only his conscious but his subconscious mind, even his sleeping mind. For, as he tells us, the world of sleep reflects and refracts 'la douleureuse synthèse de la survivance et du néant'. This remarkable episode represents, therefore, the most serious attempt ever made by a novelist to communicate, without recourse to the language of mystic symbolism, all the sensations, emotions, thoughts and even the hallucinations of a bereaved soul.

Marcel's involuntary memory of his grandmother produces an immediate sense of infinite happiness, which swiftly disappears with the realization that she is lost to him for ever. Then comes remorse, bitter and inexorable. With painful clarity, tormented by futile self-reproach, he remembers his cruel and thoughtless behaviour on that day when his grandmother had asked Saint-Loup to photograph her. She wore, to Marcel's annoyance, a wide-brimmed hat chosen deliberately, he now learns from Françoise, so as to hide the ravages of her malady. To-day, with almost masochistic tenacity, he broods on other recollections, equally painful, as if to atone thereby for the suffering he inflicted on the beloved dead one. But Marcel suggests with typical integrity that whilst he is trying to immobilize this mood, to retain its terrible intactness; whilst he is striving to remain, as it were, naked and exposed to the excruciating frozen bleakness of this spiritual climate, he becomes aware of a subtle alteration. His intelligence, that vigilant and docile servant of the instinct for self-preservation, is already at work. Thus, even when Marcel clings remorsefully to these sad images they begin to fade. He experiences a certain sweetness and serenity and recalls happier moments spent in conversation with his grandmother.

Proust has a genius for penetrative observation, for revealing, as I said, the true density of his theme. To meditate on these observations of Marcel's is to realize the fallacy of La Bruyére's 'Tout est dit' and the wisdom of Bossuet who wrote: 'Après 6000 ans d'observation, l'esprit humain n'est pas encore épuisé; il cherche, et il trouve encore afin qu'il connaisse qu'il peut trouver jusqu'à l'infini.'[2] Certainly, to some extent, Proust's originality as a novelist is due to his courage and sincerity in exploring aspects of life and morals avoided by his predecessors. But he is most profoundly original when, as in the present instance, his great talent for psychological analysis is employed to investigate experience of a more universal nature. Note, for instance, the complexity and suggestiveness of his orchestration of a theme which, in the novels of the abbé Prévost, is expressed in six words: 'il était idolâtre de sa tristesse.' And yet, Proust retains the classic quality of restraint we admire so much in Prévost and Mme de La Fayette. His pages leave ample margins for our speculation: they are always richly suggestive. Do not let us be misled by Proust's lucidity of utterance into thinking, like one of his critics, that he has no philosophy. It is not difficult to prove the superficiality of that opinion. How is it possible, for example, not to discern the philosophic implications of Marcel's observations? Here, surely, we have in essence a 'philosophy of remorse', Proust's conception of remorse as a reassertion of the human spirit, or if one may so describe it—the operation of the law of spiritual gravity which can only function, however, intermittently because it is superseded by a much stronger law: the instinct for self-preservation, 'l'ingeniosité de l'intelligence de nous préserver de la douleur'.

In this way, Marcel finds relief from the intolerable memories, deliberately invoked by himself, of the thoughtless cruelties he inflicted on his grandmother. He notes, simply, that these painful recollections were gradually replaced by gentler ones when he recalled certain of her opinions. Undoubtedly he has in mind one particular conversation in which his grandmother, disturbed by Marcel's remark that he could not possibly live without her, gently said: 'Il faut nous faire un coeur plus dur que ça. Sans cela, que deviendrais-tu si je partais en voyage?' Does Marcel now grasp the wisdom, the eternal human sadness condensed in these words? It is the tragic truth uttered by Pascal: 'Il est injuste qu'on s'attache à moi, quoiqu'on le fasse avec plaisir et volontairement. Je tromperais ceux à qui j'en ferais naître le désir, car je ne suis la fin de personne et n'ai pas de quoi les satisfaire.'[3] Always Marcel's grandmother was haunted by this thought, for she knew her grandson's insatiable craving for affection, the desolating sense of loneliness when his sensibility met with no response. Yet, because she was not a religious woman, she could not honestly imitate the example of Pascal and warn the boy that, by concentrating his tenderness upon her instead of upon God, he was doomed to be tormented, after her death, by the incomprehensible contradiction between his surviving, vivid memories of what she had meant to him and the inexorable fact that she is dead.

Notes

1. *SG*, II (1), 179.
2. *Connaissance de Dieu et de soi-même*, v, 5.
3. *Pensées* (ed. L. Brunschvieg), p. 548, *Pensées* 471.

—Frederick Charles Green, *The Mind of Proust*, (Cambridge: Cambridge University Press, 1949): 197-200.

Leo Bersani on Jealousy

[Leo Bersani is the author of *Arts of Impoverishment: Beckett, Rothko, Resnais*, and *Homos*. In this extract, he investigates the important theme of jealousy.]

But it is precisely this "mystère intime" of another person that the jealous lover tries—hopelessly and with exasperation—to penetrate. Indeed, the lover's interest is born of the anguish caused by that mystery, and needs anguish to be sustained. Now the nature of jealousy depends both on the desires of the anxious investigator and on the desires he is attempting to understand. Suffering varies according to the limits within which the loved one's desires can be imaginatively apprehended. Proust dramatizes brilliantly the ways in which the lover tries to familiarize himself with the images that appeal to the loved one, to feel how these images attract and pull the other person into certain forms of activity. The differences between particular jealousies are differences between imaginative capacities.

In the various examples of jealousy in the novel, the narrator suggests two kinds of imaginative identification with the loved one's desires that are possible for the jealous lover. Either he can identify himself with the group of people with whom the woman finds her pleasure, or he may find that, in a general way, what gives her pleasure is also what gives him pleasure. If Albertine loves Saint-Loup—and this is the "normal" jealous situation—Marcel does not share her desire, since he himself does not pursue men; but his jealousy is still bearable, because she is looking for a kind of pleasure *he can give*. The image attracting her is the image of a man, and so the nature of her desire does not absolutely exclude the possibility of Marcel's becoming the object of that desire. Her desiring glance may reflect him again, for what she sees with desire is not essentially different from his own body. The narrator insists on the fact that the idea of Albertine's having relations with other women is much more painful to him than the idea of her betraying him with Saint-Loup. The difference is one of imaginative possibility for Marcel. The jealous man, he writes, has to experiment with different kinds of suffering: "... in jealousy we have to some extent to make trial of sufferings of every sort and degree, before we arrive at the one which seems appropriate."[18] Albertine's Lesbianism is more painful to Marcel than her possible relations with men because it is more difficult for him to participate in her desires for other women: "This love of woman for woman was something too unfamiliar; nothing enabled me to form a certain, an accurate idea of its pleasures, its quality."[19]

The kind of identification Marcel can make with Albertine's Lesbian desires only aggravates his suffering. First of all, because of the pleasures he himself has known with women, he feels he has a particularly painful insight into the attractiveness of feminine images for Albertine. His own desires are being repeated, but turned against him:

> I myself, with the help of my own love of women, albeit they could not have been the same thing to Albertine, could more or less imagine what she felt. And indeed it was already a first degree of anguish, merely to picture her to myself desiring as I had so often desired, lying to me as I had so often lied to her, preoccupied with one girl or another, putting herself out for her, as I had done for Mlle. de Stermaria and ever so many others, not to mention the peasant girls whom I met on country roads. Yes, all my own desires helped me to understand, to a certain degree, what hers had been; it was by this time an intense anguish in which all my desires, the keener they had

been, had changed into torments that were all the more cruel; as though in this algebra of sensibility they reappeared with the same coefficient but with a minus instead of a plus sign.[20]

Both Marcel and Albertine are, in their desires, facing in the same direction, toward women, but there is no chance of her turning *to* him. She is, so to speak, next to him, looking at and responding to the same images as he. She wants what he wants, which is something different from him. Unable to recognize himself by analogy in what she desires (as he might have done with her desire for Saint-Loup), he has no hope of becoming the object of that desire. Moreover, although Marcel is sensitive to the attractiveness that Albertine may find in women's images, he cannot identify at all with the kind of pleasure Albertine may conceive of having with other women. They both desire women, but their bodies are satisfied in different ways. Marcel's desire for women is necessarily felt as a possibility of specific sensations, and his thoughts about Albertine's Lesbianism involve the painful paradox of finding the same images attractive but for unimaginably different reasons of physical pleasure.

NOTES

18. II, 765; *La Fugitive*, III, 546.
19. II, 649; *La Prisonnière*, III, 385.
20. II, 745–6; *La Fugitive*, III, 517.

—Leo Bersani, *Marcel Proust, The Fictions of Life and Art* (New York: Oxford University Press, 1965): 63-65.

ROGER SHATTUCK ON MARCEL'S SEXUAL RELATIONSHIP WITH ALBERTINE

[A leading expert on Proust, Roger Shattuck is Professor Emeritus of French in the Department of Modern Foreign Languages and Literatures at Boston University, and author of *Forbidden Knowledge* and *The Banquet Years*. Here he directs the reader's attention to the wryly comic aspects of Marcel's sexual relationship with Albertine through the examination of a single scene.]

Late one afternoon in Paris as Marcel lies moping on his bed, Albertine walks in unannounced. He finds her changed since the previous summer, more sophisticated. She responds to his advances, letting him kiss her. The copious yet discreet narrative implies that their caresses lead to further satisfactions, though apparently not coitus. After a long, banal conversation about mutual acquaintances and a fond good-by, Albertine leaves. Summarized in this bare form, the incident promises very little more than the commonplaces of sex. Let's see what Proust has done with it.

When Albertine walks in on him, Marcel is thinking quite lascivious thoughts, not about Albertine but about another attractive girl from Balbec from whom he expects a message that evening. Two hours later when Albertine leaves, Marcel will not commit himself to a time to see her again. The other girl is still very much on his mind, and he wants to keep his time open. Thus the scene is framed in carnal desire, but carefully deflected so that Albertine's entrance comes both as a total surprise and as perfectly appropriate to the mood.

We are reminded, however, that when Marcel first tried to make a pass at Albertine the previous summer in what looked like a perfect setup in his hotel room, she literally pulled the cord on him and rang for help. Will she respond now? The real question, the old refrain of every unexpected or long-delayed encounter with her, is: who is Albertine? Marcel stumbles about among sensual memories of Albertine in Balbec and present realities. "I don't know whether what took possession of me at that moment was a desire for Balbec or for her" (II, 351). He decides in any case that he is not in love with Albertine and wants no more than a simple, peaceful satisfaction from her presence.

But now he notices her language, the expressions she calmly produces from the new "social treasure" she has accumulated since the previous summer. Marcel makes a number of "philological discoveries" about her vocabulary. They provide the "evidence of certain upheavals, the nature of which was unknown to me, but sufficient to justify me in all my hopes" (II, 356). Marcel is indeed reading Albertine like a book.

> "*To my mind* [Albertine said], that's the best thing that could possibly happen. I regard it as the perfect solution, the stylish way out."
>
> All this was so novel, so manifestly an alluvial deposit leading one to suspect such capricious wanderings over terrain hitherto unknown to her, that, on hearing the words "to my mind," I drew her down on the bed beside me (II, 356).

Marcel has interpreted the signs correctly. If one is familiar with the way Proust moves calmly away from such moments and continues as if from another planet, the next sentences will come naturally.

> No doubt it does happen that women of moderate culture, on marrying well-read men, receive such expressions as part of their dowry. And shortly after the metamorphosis which follows the wedding night, when they start paying calls....

The sentence goes on for twenty lines. Having succeeded in maneuvering Albertine onto the bed, Marcel has wits enough about him only to try the "I'm not ticklish" approach. Albertine cooperates and, as they shift into position, asks considerately if she isn't too heavy. Then it happens.

> As she uttered these words, the door opened and Françoise, carrying a lamp, walked in.

Albertine scrambles back to a chair. It is not clear whether Françoise has been following every move from outside the door or is simply bringing in the lamp at the usual hour. In the two-page examination of this interruption, we learn that Françoise's smallest actions constitute a moral language inflicting her code of values on everyone around her. She emerges convincingly from the analysis as the mythological figure of "Justice Shedding Light on Crime." Caught practically *in flagrante delicto*, Marcel tries to carry it off.

> "What? the lamp already? Heavens, how bright it is." My object, as may be imagined, was by the second of these exclamations to account for my confusion, and by the first to excuse my slow reactions. Françoise replied with cruel ambiguity, "Do you want me to sniff it out?"

> "... snuff?" Albertine murmured in my ear, leaving me charmed by the lively familiarity with which, taking me at once for master and accomplice, she insinuated this psychological affirmation in the form of a grammatical question (II, 360).[2]

When Françoise leaves, Albertine is ready for action again. But not so Marcel. There is a precedent. Swann, about to kiss Odette, tries to delay things in order to take full cognizance of what is happening. (See the passage quoted in the note on p. 26.) He senses something momentous and final in the act they are about to perform. Marcel holds off for similar reasons, about which we learn in some detail. Unhurriedly he rehearses the successive stages of their acquaintance and tries to reconstruct "this little girl's novel"—that is, her life beyond his ken. Knowing that it is now possible to kiss Albertine means more to Marcel than acting on the opportunity; his principal concern seems to be to breathe back into her person all the "mystery" she once carried so that, in kissing her cheeks, he will be kissing "the whole Balbec beach" (II, 363). Next comes a short disquisition on kissing and the dubious prospect of knowing anything by lip contact. We are now fifteen pages and probably an hour's reading time into the scene, and there would seem to be no way of spinning things out much longer. Marcel has her where he wants her, except that the old refrain never ceases: who is Albertine? I quote with only a few cuts.

> To begin with, as my mouth began gradually to approach the cheeks which my eyes had tempted it to kiss, my eyes, in changing position saw a different pair of cheeks; the throat, studied at closer range and as though through a magnifying glass, showed a coarser grain and a robustness which modified the character of the face.
>
> Apart from the most recent applications of the art of photography—which can set crouching at the foot of a cathedral all the houses, which time and time again, when we stood near them, appeared to reach almost the height of towers.... [ten more lines on photography] I can think of nothing that can so effectively as a kiss evoke out of what we believed to be a thing with one definite appearance, the hundred other things which it may equally well be, since each is related to a no less legiti-

> mate view of it. In short, just as at Balbec Albertine had often appeared different to me, so now ... [here seven lines to say that such slow motion really serves to pass very rapidly in review all the different impressions one has had of a person] ... during this brief passage of my lips toward her cheek, it was ten Albertines that I saw; she was like a goddess with several heads, and whenever I sought to approach one of them, it was replaced by another. At least so long as I had not touched her head, I could still see it, and a faint perfume reached me from it. But alas—for in this business of kissing our nostrils and eyes are as ill-placed as our lips are ill-shaped—suddenly my eyes ceased to see; next, my nose, crushed by the collision, no longer perceived any fragrance, and, without thereby gaining any clearer idea of the taste of the rose of my desire, I learned from these unpleasant signs, that at last I was in the act of kissing Albertine's cheek (II, 364–65).

Notice, among other things, that it is never directly recorded in the testimony given here that Marcel kisses Albertine. At the crucial moment, he literally loses his senses. She vanishes. Consciousness cannot track experience to its lair. It must wait outside while another being, blind but active, performs a deed that the consciousness then reconstructs *ex post facto* from flimsy evidence. The question "Who is Albertine?" pales to triviality beside its counterpart: "Who am *I*?" But here Proust has done two things simultaneously. He has shown how sheer awareness, self-reflexiveness, erodes the reality of any action, even, or rather particularly, when we attach great significance to it; and he has written a superb pastiche of his own style, a savage-sympathetic blow-up of all the gestures with which he usually introduces us to reality and its bitter disappointments. The relaxed reader can be amused both by Marcel's resounding defeat of his own purposes *as he achieves them*, and the Narrator's detachment from his own involuted narrative.

This "Kissing Albertine" sequence will bear sustained scrutiny. Most obviously, it dramatizes the dissociation of love, an idealized sentiment created by the imagination, from desire, focused on a material object. The passage also hints at Marcel's great yearning, in the midst of jealousies and disappointments, for the peaceable kingdom. He hopes Albertine will calm his life as his mother and grandmother were able to do. But few moments of serenity will in fact come from this budding affair. The action here echoes several other themes: the power of language to influence thought, the intermittent quality of character and identity, and the ironic timing of important events in our lives. But more important than this disparate content is the fact that all of it fuses not into a romantic or erotic scene but into a primarily comic incident. There is no element in the scene that fails to contribute to the mood of self-mockery leading to open laughter.

This is the shortest of the four sequences that turn Marcel's life toward the long plateau of maturity. It will be revealing to look at the other three in reverse order.

At the evening reception at the Prince and Princesse de Guermantes's sumptuous *hôtel particulier*, Marcel attains his social ambitions and, through one hundred fifty pages, observes the inflated emptiness and corruption of that society. The description of the characters recalls Daumier and even George Grosz. The Due de Guermantes's crinkly hair, when he is angry, "seems to come out of a crater" (II, 683). The Marquise de Citry is "still beautiful, but barely suppressing a death rattle" ("*encore belle, mais presque l'écume aux dents*") (II, 687). The comic element here is no mere matter of applied detail. From the start Marcel suspects that the invitation he has received to this chic affair is a hoax, and that he will be turned away at the door. His attempts to track down the origin of his invitation lead nowhere. Yet he cannot stay away. It gradually builds up to one of the great drolleries in Proust. The scene begins with an elaborate preparatory sequence about the head footman having been picked up the night before by an anonymous and generous gentleman who was in fact the Duc de Châtellerault. As it happens the Duke is just ahead of Marcel in line as they wait to have their names belted out to the guests by this same, now imposing footman. When the footman learns, from the man's own lips, his anonymous lover's identity, he "shouts [it] out with truly professional gusto tinged with intimate tenderness." Marcel now totters forward. His fears about the spuriousness of his invitation to this prestigious event have been built up for pages. I can only quote.

> But now it was my turn to be announced. Absorbed in contemplation of my hostess, who had not yet seen me, I had not thought of the function—terrible to me, although not in the same sense as to M. de Châtellerault—of this footman garbed in black like an executioner, surrounded by a group of lackeys in the most cheerful livery, stout fellows ready to seize hold of an intruder and cast him out. The footman asked me my name, I told it to him as mechanically as the condemned man allows himself to be strapped to the block. Straightening up he lifted his majestic head and, before I could beg him to announce me in a lowered tone so as to spare my own feelings if I were not invited and those of the Princesse de Guermantes if I were, shouted the disturbing syllables with a force capable of shaking the very vaulting in the ceiling.
>
> The famous Huxley (whose grandson occupies an unassailable position in the English literary world of today) relates that one of his patients stopped going out socially because often, on the actual chair that was pointed out to her with a courteous gesture, she saw an old gentleman already seated. She could be quite certain that either the gesture of invitation or the old gentleman's presence was a hallucination, for her hostess would not have offered her a chair that was already occupied. And when Huxley, to cure her, forced her to reappear in society, she felt a moment of painful hesitation when she asked herself if the friendly sign that was being made to her was the real thing, or if, in obedience to a nonexistent vision, she was about to sit down in public upon the knees of a flesh-and-blood gentleman. Her brief uncertainty was agonizing. Less so perhaps than mine. After the sound of my name, like the rumble that warns us of a possible cataclysm, I was bound, at least in order to plead my own good faith, and as though I were not tormented by any doubts, to advance toward the Princess with a resolute air.
>
> She caught sight of me when I was still a few feet away and (in an action that left no further doubt about my being the victim of a conspiracy) instead of remaining seated, as she had done for her other guests, rose and came toward me. A moment later I was able to heave the sigh of relief of Huxley's patient, who, having made up her mind to sit down in the

chair, found it vacant and realized that it was the old gentleman who was the hallucination. The Princess had just held out her hand to me with a smile (II, 637–38).

Proust narrates the incident with a precision of timing and flourish worthy of an acrobat balanced on top of a thirty-foot stack of tables. Twice he lets us think he is going to fall, first when he allows the Duke's subplot to take over, and later when he interrupts the story at the climax with the tantalizing Huxley digression. But he never loses control, and the story inches on. Basically Proust draws his effects here out of the double I. The enigmatic appearance of all unfamiliar things fills Marcel with anxiety and the Narrator with amusement. The resultant text shows us hallucination playing chase with perception, danger with detachment. We smile or chuckle each time the acrobat comes close to falling, though we remain apprehensive. After this opening, it is hard not to look for comedy in the rest of the scene.

Note

2. Moncrieff translated Françoise's faulty subjunctive, "*Faut-il que j'éteinde*?" as "Do you want me to extinguish it?" Albertine supplies, "—guish!"

—Roger Shattuck, *Marcel Proust*, (Princeton: Princeton University Press, 1974): 58-65.

Patrick Brady on Introversion and Narcissism

[Patrick Brady has taught at Rice and Harvard Universities, and currently holds the Shumway Chair for Excellence at the University of Tennessee at Knoxville. In this passage, he uncovers the narcissistic underpinnings of much of the sexual inversion in the novel.]

Inversion is a major theme of the work, a preoccupation which is reflected in the title of *Cities of the Plain* (*Sodome et Gomorrhe*). Homosexuals of both sexes are portrayed: pederasts like M. de

Charlus, Prince Gilbert de Guermantes, M. de Vaugoubert, Nissim Bernard, Legrandin, Robert de Saint-Loup, and the objects of their affection—Jupien, Morel, Theodore, and others; lesbians like Mlle. Vinteuil and her friend, Lea the actress, Bloch's cousin, probably Andrée, and Albertine.

This theme of inversion is explicitly related to that of introversion (a much more common and anodine psychological phenomenon, of course) in a passage in which Albertine indicates, "set in the wall in front of us, a large mirror which I had not noticed and upon which I now realised that my friend, while talking to me, had never ceased to fix her troubled, preoccupied eyes."[45] In this mirror Albertine has been exchanging glances with two lesbians. The essential character of homosexuality, moreover, is well symbolized by the mirror, for the invert is attracted by the alter ego character of the objects of his or her attention. The mirror also symbolizes mere introversion. There is not conclusive evidence that the protagonist is a homosexual, but inversion is closely related to introversion, and the narrator is certainly quite introverted. In spite of his active social life, he very often expresses a strong preference for solitude. It leads him to condemn friendship, whose whole aim, he asserts, is to get us to sacrifice to a superficial self the only *real* part of ourselves, which cannot be communicated except through art. He compares the temptation of friendship to that of a pointless cause for which an artist, afraid of seeming or possibly being selfish, gives his life instead of living for the masterpiece which he bears within him.

In such passages, the narrator is concerned with solitude as a condition for creativity: "Robert having finished giving his instructions to the driver joined me now in the carriage. The ideas that had appeared before me took flight. Ideas are goddesses who deign at times to make themselves visible to a solitary mortal, at a turning in the road, even in his bedroom while he sleeps, when they, standing framed in the doorway, bring him the annunciation of their tidings. But as soon as a companion joins him they vanish, in the society of his fellows no man has ever beheld them. And I found myself cast back upon friendship."[46] Like Robert de Saint-Loup, Albertine threatens the precious solitude of the protagonist: she is a perpetual presence, greedy for movement and life, which disturbs his sleep, ever leaving doors open for him to catch cold, and forcing him to invent reasons for not accompanying her on outings. In particular, her mere presence prevents him from experiencing certain pleasures: whereas she feels her pleasure at seeing certain monuments would be increased by seeing them with him, he believes he could neither give nor feel any pleasure at seeing them unless he visited them alone or at least pretended to be alone. Solitude is essential: "Albertine admired, and by her presence prevented me from admiring, the reflections of red sails upon the wintry blue of the water."[47] Thus the most precious of both active and passive functions, that is, of both artistic creation and aesthetic pleasure, are dependent, for the protagonist, on solitude.

To this theme of introversion we may relate that of narcissism, of which we need give only a partial indication at this point. He asserts that he is modest enough to seek to hide his good qualities, speaking of "the people in whose company I have succeeded in concealing most effectively the slight advantages a knowledge of which might have given them a less derogatory idea of myself";[48] later he claims to be so modest that he is not even aware of these qualities: "I realised that the Guermantes did indeed regard me as being of another race, but one that aroused their envy because I possessed merits of which I knew nothing and which they professed to regard as alone important."[49] The "insincerity" betrayed by the inconsistency between such statements is revealed on other occasions as well: after admitting that he is "the least courageous of men,"[50] he will later declare that, "I had never been timid, I had been easily led into duels,"[51] and denies any fear of the shells and bombs falling on Paris during World War I. A further inconsistency is associated with his grandmother. (It is in connection with her memory that he blames his symbiotic hypersensitivity for inspiring in him a cowardly refusal to face cruelty and injustice.) He declares that like her he is unable to judge others or bear grudges and is free from vanity and pride, as from self-respect (*amour-propre*), but his own self-portrait betrays great vanity and pride (in the form of narcissism, snobbery, and so on), and at least one important form of *amour-propre* admitted to quite explicitly and at great length: that which involves risking danger in order to retain another's high opinion of him and of his noble and favorable disposition.

The theme of impotence is evoked in connection with M. d'Argencourt, who abandons his wife for a young socialite but finds her sexually difficult to satisfy. What of the protagonist himself? He speaks several times of having possessed Albertine and of being her lover—and indeed of having had other mistresses. In fact, he is inclined to boast of the number of his conquests: "I must confess that many of her friends—I was not yet in love with her—gave me, at one watering-place or another, moments of pleasure. These obliging young comrades did not seem to me to be very many. But recently I have thought it over, their names have recurred to me. I counted that, in that one season, a dozen conferred on me their ephemeral favours. A name came back to me later, which made thirteen. I then, with almost a child's delight in cruelty, dwelt upon that number. Alas, I realised that I had forgotten the first of them all, Albertine who no longer existed and who made the fourteenth."[52]

Nevertheless, several indications suggest that intercourse is beyond him, psychologically if not physically. The key passage here is the following, which dilutes drastically the meaning to be attributed to the term "lover" claimed elsewhere by the narrator: "Albertine alarmed me further when she said that I was quite right to say, out of regard for her reputation, that I was not her lover, since 'for that matter,' she went on, 'it's perfectly true that you aren't.' I was not her lover perhaps in the full sense of the word, but then, was I to suppose that all the things that we did together she did also with all the other men whose mistress she swore to me that she had never been?"[53] From this passage we may deduce that the protagonist has not actually had sexual intercourse with Albertine. Such a hypothesis would explain her desire for relations with a man, as expressed in the exclamation "Thank you for nothing! Fancy spending a cent upon those old frumps, I'd a great deal rather you left me alone for once in a way so that I can go and get some one decent to break my [pot]."[54] The narrator comments as follows: "Horror! It was this that she would have preferred. Two-fold horror! For even the vilest of prostitutes, who consents to that sort of thing, or desires it, does not employ to the man who yields to her desires that appalling expression. She would feel the degradation too great. To a woman alone, if she loves women, she says this, as an excuse for giving herself presently to a man."[55] It is striking that he twice describes his own orgasm, once with Gilberte and once with Albertine, but never that of his partner, who seems to be thus reduced (like the reader) to the role of spectator.

It is possible, on the other hand, that the protagonist, who is capable of orgasm and is therefore not really impotent, simply has no taste for the consummation of sexual relations with a woman—which brings us back to our starting point: inversion. Such a hypothesis would explain a number of other elements of the work, including the protagonist's striking resemblance with one of the female characters: "At that moment I caught sight of myself in the mirror; I was struck by a certain resemblance between myself and Andrée. If I had not long since ceased to shave my upper lip and had had but the faintest shadow of a moustache, the resemblance would have been almost complete."[56]

Another significant resemblance is that between the protagonist and M. de Charlus. If the latter is always on the side of the weak, so is the protagonist; the latter's identification of individuals with the village and the countryside to which they belong reappears in Charlus; the particular form of selfishness shown by the protagonist toward Albertine recurs in Charlus' treatment of Morel. And whereas there is some evidence, as I have indicated, that the protagonist may be psychologically incapable of intercourse (at least with women), Charlus is obsessed with a dream of virility. These resemblances would then explain the narrator's keen appreciation of Charlus. The most striking of them is the similarity between Charlus' relationship with his protégé (sketched with the protagonist and carried out with Morel) and the protagonist's relationship with his protégée Albertine. Other elements then come to mind: the fact that the protagonist's preference goes to a girl like Albertine, who first strikes him as athletic and is finally described as being "masculine"[57] and the counterpart of Charlus: "it was perhaps, I told myself, Albertine's vice itself, the cause of my future sufferings, that had produced in her that honest, frank manner, creating the illusion that one could enjoy with her the same loyal and unrestricted comradeship as with a man, just as a parallel vice had produced in M. de Charlus a feminine refinement of sensibility and mind."[58]

The protagonist reveals an apparent passivity in his physical relations with the opposite sex. Thus to express his desire for Albertine he invites her to tickle him! She will not let him kiss her except when, as he says, "it was I, now, who was lying in bed and she who sat beside me, capable of evading any brutal attack and of dictating her pleasure to me."[59] The transparent request to be tickled occurs again later, this time with a servant, whom he tells to search him (in the dark: he has blown out the candle) for money. His passivity with Albertine is fairly constant: generally, she controls the situation, whether preventing his action or taking the initiative herself. He experiences Albertine's kiss "like a penetration."[60]

To the narrator, with his passion for the study of abnormal psychological states, we may well apply his own comment: "What specialist in the insane has not, as a result of spending time with them, had his attack of insanity? In fact he is lucky if he can affirm that it was not a previous, latent insanity that had moved him to work with them. The object of a psychiatrist's studies often reacts on him. But before that, what obscure inclination, what fascinating fear had made him choose that object?"[61] It is true that he tries to persuade us that the abnormal psychology he studies is in fact normal, at least in the sense of being universal in human nature: "When a living being—and perhaps in nature that creature is man—is so poorly constituted that he cannot love without suffering and must suffer in order to learn new truths...."[62] But this is not particularly persuasive.

His taste for little girls, which gets him into trouble with the police for corrupting a minor, is a pathetic way for him to end, with a request that Gilberte supply him with new ones; it tends to support the view that his own psychological makeup is something less than normal.

45. *CP*, I, 283 (*Pl*, II, 803).
46. *GW*, II, 124 (*Pl*, II, 398).
47. *C*, 231 (*Pl*, III, 174).
48. *WBG*, II, 212 (*Pl*, I, 853).
49. *GW*, II, 180 (*Pl*, II, 439).
50. *WBG*, II, 212 (*Pl*, I, 853).
51. *C*, 393 (*Pl*, III, 291).
52. *CP*, I, 265 (*Pl*, II, 789).
53. *C*, 123 (*Pl*, III, 97).
54. *C*, 463 (*Pl*, III, 338).
55. *C*, 466 (*Pl*, III, 340–41).
56. *SCG*, 183 (*Pl*, III, 549).
57. *SCG*, 313 (*Pl*, III, 643).
58. *SCG*, 268 (*Pl*, III, 611).
59. *GW*, II, 77 (*Pl*, II, 365).
60. *SCC*, 113 (*Pl*, III, 498).
61. Passage missing from Scott-Moncrieff but included in the Pléïade edition, III, 206–7.
62. *PR*, 240–41 (*Pl*, III, 909).

—Patrick Brady, *Marcel Proust*, (Boston: Twayne Publishers, 1977): 26-30.

JACK MURRAY ON CHARLUS AS A COMEDIC CHARACTER

[Here, Murray describes the scene in which Marcel eavesdrops on Charlus and Jupien.]

The most exotically described sexual ritual in the novel, however, is Charlus's encounter with Jupien in the courtyard of the Hotel de Guermantes. The dominant metaphoric framework in which the encounter is placed is that of the insect bringing just the right pollen to the tropical plant the Duchess de Guermantes has placed outside her apartment in hopes that it may be fertilized. The encounter between Charlus and Jupien is seen as just as miraculous since Jupien happens to be one of those rare homosexuals who is attracted by older men. Since this event has been so often analyzed, there is little need to review it here in any detail. What is of most concern in the present chapter is sexual comedy itself. Therefore, for our immediate purposes, the most interesting aspect of the episode is the routine into which both men fall when they first set eyes on each other and register mutual sexual attraction.

> But, more astounding still, M. de Charlus's attitude having changed, Jupien's, as though in obedience to the laws of an occult art, at once brought itself into harmony with it. The Baron, who was now seeking to conceal the impression that had been made on him, and yet, in spite of his affectation of indifference, seemed unable to move away without regret, went, came, looked vaguely into the distance in the way which, he felt, most enhanced the beauty of his eyes, assumed a complacent, careless, fatuous air. Meanwhile Jupien, shedding at once the humble, honest expression which I had always associated with him, had—in perfect symmetry with the Baron—thrown up his head, given a becoming tilt to his body, placed his hand with a grotesque impertinence on his hip, stuck out his behind, posed himself with the coquetry that the orchid might have adopted on the providential arrival of the bee. (CP, 5–6; RTP, II, 604)

Because the two persons involved in this flirtation are of the same sex, Proust could easily have contented himself with leaving this scene in the domain of burlesque comedy. One thinks of a parody of Carmen meeting Don José. But the author wishes to draw our attention to the bizarre quality of the scene as well: "This scene was not, however, positively comic, it was stamped with a strangeness, or if you like a naturalness the beauty of which steadily increased" (CP, 6; RTP, II, 605). In short, Proust wants us to approach what happens from an aesthetic standpoint as well. Here we have one of many instances of how closely the aesthetic and the comic are allied in Proust's thinking. And, once more, what transpires takes on a theatrical aspect: "Certainly, the affairs of this sort of which I have been a spectator have always been presented in a setting of the most imprudent and least probable character" (CP, 8; RTP, II, 608). Moreover, the comic tone becomes dominant once the sexual transaction has taken place and the two men engage in "shop-talk" about homosexual topics. Charlus, for example, begins to discuss other attractive men he has noticed in the neighborhood about whom he is curious, apparently oblivious to the feelings of Jupien who reproaches him with a rather silly "I can see you [*have the heart of an artichoke*]" (CP, 9; RTP, II, 609). The baron also launches into an involved account of his pursuit of a trolley car operator. Finally, as is his wont, Charlus refers metaphorically to his "august bishop's mantle" (CP, 11; RTP, II, 612) which throws the literal-minded Jupien into a momentary fluster. Plainly, Proust wishes us to understand this scene in predominantly comic terms.

The scene, however, which appears to epitomize all love scenes in *Remembrance of Things Past* is Charlus's torture on the rack in Jupien's male bordello in *The Past Recaptured*. With as much plausibility as in the Montjouvain scene, Marcel just happens by as the scene occurs. He is in the hotel, which he has entered by accident in hope of finding something to drink, and hears muffled cries coming from somewhere within. Eventually he finds the room from which the cries are issuing and climbs up to a convenient transom from which he observes Charlus chained to the bed and being beaten by a tough brandishing whip, a leather whip with nails in it. A dialogue is in progress, the very exaggeration of which suggests melodrama. Charlus is saying, "I beseech you, mercy, have pity, untie me, don't beat me so hard." His tormentor Maurice replies, "No, you filthy brute ... and if you yell and drag yourself about on your knees like that you'll be tied to the bed, no mercy for you" (PR, 90–91; RTP, III, 815). All of this is accompanied by lashings from the scourge, and Marcel notices that the baron's back bears the hideous traces of previous beatings. These marks indicate the ritual aspect of what is taking place and confirm our earlier idea that the scene at Montjouvain is also a ritual that has been played out many times before Marcel accidentally observes it. Charlus's torture might be described in theatrical terms just as much as the earlier scene, particularly since Charlus, at one point, asks Maurice to leave the room and then complains to Jupien that he is not convincing enough in his part. In this way, Proust insists on the play-acting involved in the sadist–masochist relationship and raises the question, certainly comic here, of whether one may speak of good or bad acting in such a situation.

The narrator notes a resemblance between Maurice (or the substitute sent to replace him) and Morel, the great love of Charlus's life, one who would correspond to what Odette is for Swann or Albertine for Marcel. It is as if Charlus, who has long separated from Morel, were still seeking to suffer from him through proxies who, by beating him, play Morel's role at once too symbolically and too literally. Yet Marcel's discovery of the resemblance between the baron's present torturer and Morel contributes nothing toward clearing up the mystery, as the author describes it, but only deepens it, since Morel himself may be some primordial archetype lurking as a continuum in Charlus's unconscious. This suggestion of infinite regress heightens the repetitive sense we have of a ritual or dramatic performance that has been played out so many times that the players themselves have lost all notion of the sense of it and simply continue to repeat the words and gestures in a futile effort to revive forgotten feelings and dimly remembered purposes.

The futility of Charlus's efforts at sensational self-chastisement is perhaps also a comment on Marcel's affairs, or Swann's, in which a somewhat more subtle form of self-torture is involved. The vanity of Marcel's attempts to win possession of Gilberte or Albertine is thereby emphasized all the more. A single affair, described in the framework, say, of Swann's love for Odette, might have made the phenomenon seem isolated. But because it is repeated in an increasingly tormented form, culminating in the raw and brutal masochism of Charlus's self-chastisement in Jupien's bordello, it comes to be a particularly appalling and, at the same time, saddening variation of the Proustian comedy.[9] The final picture we have is of all humanity struggling to win that impossible reward—possession of another person—, and, in the process, falling into the trap of self-punishment as each one realizes the hopeless isolation in which he lives. This is the cream of every sexual joke in the novel.

In conclusion, it is possible to see homosexual relationships as parodies of normal ones and also as epitomes of all love. Since love is based on illusion, Jupien's feminine strut in front of Charlus is no more misleading than the eyes a flirtatious lady might make at an attractive gentleman, yet it does bring out the bizarre comedy of the whole phenomenon of sexual attraction. True, Charlus sees an effeminate man, and not a female, as he looks at Jupien, just as Swann continues to see Odette as a shallow and stupid woman. The physical person is merely a point of departure for the return to some erotic image that may have lain dormant for a time in the lover's mind. Charlus best illustrates this, as he passes from Morel-substitute to Morel-substitute. Similarly, few readers will fail to note the great similarities between Gilberte and Albertine, and it is by no means fair to attribute these to Proust's insufficient skill as a novelist.

Proustian love is relentlessly oriented toward private suffering. It is always misplaced, always one-sided, always punished. The homosexual interludes in the novel emphasize that the self-chastisement, which seems a rather accidental, or simply unfortunate, aspect of normal love as depicted in the novel, is perhaps quite deliberate and even the main goal on the lover's part. This is most explicitly the case with Charlus when on the rack at Jupien's. But it is quite plainly a dominant element in Mlle. Vinteuil's scene with her friend at Montjouvain. These scenes shed light on Swann's relentless scrutiny of Odette's present and past for all their sordid and tawdry adventures, to say nothing of Marcel's similar enterprises that he engages in over Albertine.

Proust's stress on the animal aspect of the sexual urge tends to make us conceive of all the rest in plainly Baudelarian terms. And, as with Baudelaire, the irresistible sexual urge, tied as it is with degradation and the humiliation that comes from our sordid physicality, produces a bitter sort of comedy. The sexual impulse, and its attendant pleasure, is not something that is shared, in blissful physical communion, with the partner in either Proust or Baudelaire. Instead, each partner makes wretched, even devouring, use of the other, so that contempt and cruelty seem its most dominant characteristics.[10]

It is our own observation that homosexual love, in Proust, is a parody on normal love and that, like all parodies, it makes certain grotesque aspects of normal love more explicit. It is Proust himself, however, who continually stresses the role of acting in love. On the more ordinary level, we have simply the feigned indifference of the lover who does not want his feelings to be understood too soon, or the flirtatiousness of the woman anxious to catch the lover. We have also the acting required by the mistress when she resorts to lying, the acting of the lover when he tries to find out the truth. On a higher level, we have the lover who attempts to hide his suffering or else to divert it—for example, when Marcel acts as if he does not love Gilberte anymore. But, on the highest level, we have Proust's introduction of melodrama when it almost comes to seem as if what is at stake is suffering for suffering's own sake. Mlle. Vinteuil is an "artist in evil," and her ceremony with her friend possesses a scenario, a whole ritual, that conforms to the outline of some vast structure of violence and suffering inside the tortured young woman. The squalid and pathetic imperfections in the drama as it is clumsily acted out by the two women only point up all the more the deep design that attempts to make itself felt through their fumbling gestures. It is, in fact, some primal drama, repeated again and again in the novel, that emerges to haunt them, just as it will visit the life of every character sooner or later. Such a primal drama is embodied in melodrama itself, and it is now time to turn to this central topic.

Notes

9. See Marcel M. Gutwirth, "Le Portrait de Charlus dans l'oeuvre de Proust," *Romanic Review*, XL, no. 3 (Oct., 1949), p. 180.

10. See René Galand, "Proust et Baudelaire," *PMLA*, LXV, no. 6 (Dec., 1960), pp. 1026–1027.

—Jack Murray, *The Proustian Comedy*, (York, South Carolina: French Literature Publications Company, 1980): 88-92.

J. E. Rivers on The Extended Essay on "Inversion"

[J.E. Rivers is Professor at the University of Colorado, Boulder, and co-editor of *Nabokov's Fifth Arc*. In this extract, Rivers, gives a detailed evaluation of the first section of *Cities of the Plain*.]

The narrator's distinction between classical and modern homosexuality[45] is perhaps best illustrated by comparing the history of a typical boy with homosexual tastes as given in *Sodome I* with the history given by Aristophanes in Plato's *Symposium*, a work with which, as we have seen, Proust was familiar. Whether intentionally or not, the narrator's scheme reverses Aristophanes' at practically every point. In the two characterizations, such youths:

Aristophanes	*Proust's narrator*
Are fond of men while young and take joy in lying with and embracing them	Mistake the first stirrings of desire when pressing against a comrade for the mutual desire for a woman
Are the best of boys, the bravest, the most manly	Are shy, withdrawn, effeminate
Are open about their desires, often to the point of being called shameless	Are forced to conceal their desires, meet in the dark
Grow up to be men of public affairs	Often lead solitary, lonely lives
Tend to reject the idea of marriage to women in favor of living unmarried together	Live hypocritical lives and pretend they are attracted to women; if lucky enough to find a partner, they are likely to lose him when the partner marries a woman
Delight in the company of those that are like them	Often shun each other's company out of shame and self-hatred[46]

And so on. In the narrator's presentation modern homosexuality, as a psychological illness, is for its victims as ineluctable, as inescapable, as cruel in its onsets and false remissions as the grandmother's dreadful physical ailment—whose pattern, moreover it follows (withdrawal, loneliness, suffering, attempts at concealment, rejection by those who should be the most concerned, gradual degeneration of the personality). The outlook is dark, to be sure, but is brightened somewhat in ways we shall consider presently.

Homosexuality in *A la recherche* is a sociological as well as a psychological phenomenon. Proust works into the novel the idea, widespread at the time and much talked about during the Eulenburg affair, that people with homosexual tastes comprise a special subclass of society—"a freemasonry," as the narrator phrases it, "much more widespread, more efficacious and less suspected than that of the lodges ... within which the members ... recognize each other by signs which are natural or conventional, voluntary or involuntary" (2: 617). It is a society which extends across all the earth, "having adherents everywhere, among the common people, in the army, in the temple, in prison, on the throne," a society whose members can be found "in London, in Berlin, in Rome, in Petrograd, or in Paris" (2: 617, 632). Here it is easy to see how the ideas, the imagery, even the enumerative, distributive style derive from writing on homosexuality contemporary with Proust. Both style and substance were commonplace, whether the writer was interested in denouncing homosexuality, defending it, or giving an objective, scientific evaluation. John Addington Symonds wrote in 1891 that homosexuality "confronts us on the steppes of Asia ... in the bivouac of Keltish warriors ... upon the sands of Arabia .... among the palm groves of the South Sea Islands ... under Eskimos' snow-huts; beneath the sultry vegetation of Peru, ... It throbs in our huge cities. The pulse of it can be felt in London, Paris, Berlin, Vienna, no less than in Constantinople, Naples, Teheran, and Moscow."[47] Similarly, the German physician Casper reported that homosexuality is to be found "on the Rigi, at Palermo, in the Louvre, in the Highlands of Scotland, in Petersburg, at the port of Barcelona."[48] Casper, Tarnowsky, and the Italian sexologist Mantegazza mentioned the arcane signs and signals people with homosexual preferences supposedly use to recognize each other.[49] And well before Proust, Richard

Burton, Edward Carpenter, and Maximilian Harden compared the subsociety of homosexuality to freemasonry.[50] Harden wrote that men with homosexual inclinations form "a comradeship which is stronger than that of ... freemasonry, which ... unites the most remote, the most foreign, in a fraternal league of offence and defence. Men of this breed are to be found everywhere, at Courts, in high positions in armies and navies, in the editorial offices of great newspapers, at tradesmen's and teachers' desks, even on the Bench. All rally together against the common enemy."[51]

Harden's idea that homosexually oriented people are united in a worldwide conspiracy having evil designs on the rest of humanity is echoed in *A la recherche*. The narrator also envisions a homosexual conspiracy, equating it metaphorically with the Jewish or Zionist conspiracy about which so much had been heard during the Dreyfus affair. He avers that people with homosexual tastes proselytize for their cause with a zeal comparable to that of Zionists, draft-dodgers, Saint-Simonians, vegetarians, and anarchists (2: 620; cf. 632). He says that such people live "in an endearing and dangerous intimacy with men of the other race, provoking them ... until the day of scandal when these subduers are themselves devoured" (2: 617). In *La Prisonnière* the narrator describes two women who go out, with one of them dressed as a man, for the purpose of picking up children and "initiating" them into the homosexual way of life (3: 351). And later in the novel Andrée says that Morel had a special arrangement with Albertine whereby he used his attractiveness to women to lure young girls into lesbian adventures with her. "Once he had the audacity," Andrée continues, "to take Albertine and one of these girls into a house of ill repute at Couliville, where four or five of the women had her together or in succession. That was his passion, as it was also Albertine's" (3: 600). Thus do male and female adherents of homosexuality join forces to corrupt the youth of France.

The idea that "homosexuals" conspire against and attempt to seduce the people "of the other race" is one of the hoariest myths surrounding homosexuality. It is, as we have seen, a myth Proust exposes and satirizes in the conflict between Charlus and Mme

Verdurin and in the encounter between Charlus and Cottard in the scene of the sham duel. And yet in other sections of the novel Proust allows his narrator to advance this bit of prejudice as if it were the general truth, to write, indeed, as if he were taking his inspiration directly from Maximilian Harden. The narrator decides that Albertine hid her lesbianism from him "like a woman who might have hidden from me that she was a spy from an enemy nation, and more treacherously even than a spy, because a spy deceives only with respect to her nationality, whereas with Albertine the deception had to do with her most profound humanity" (3: 527). Although the primary purpose of this image is to emphasize the mystery of Albertine's identity, it depends upon and endorses the traditional equation of homosexuality with treason and conspiracy. And in other sections of the novel the narrator pushes the idea as far as it will go by suggesting that people with homosexual inclinations, when given a chance, will aggressively seduce other people, whether children or adults, into the homosexual way of life.

Sex researchers tell us, however, that the seduction of children is extremely rare among homosexually oriented people and is, in fact, principally a heterosexual practice.[52] And there are, of course, no more grounds for believing in a homosexual conspiracy than there are for believing in a Jewish conspiracy. In 1927 Magnus Hirschfeld perceptively wrote: "It is untrue that homosexuals form a sort of 'secret society' among themselves with all sorts of code signals and mutual defense arrangements. Aside from a few minor cliques, homosexuals are in reality almost totally lacking in feelings of solidarity; in fact, it would be difficult to find another class of mankind which has proved so incapable of organizing to secure its basic legal and human rights."[53] Recently, of course, the homosexual liberation movement has made significant gains in securing civil rights for people with a homosexual orientation. But the point, which should be obvious to anyone who reflects for a moment, is that homosexually oriented people do not organize or communicate with each other any more regularly or any more skillfully than other classes of people. True, they have an argot referring to various sexual attitudes and practices. But so do heterosexually oriented people, and in many instances the argot is the same. Proust's narrator's assertion that people with homosexual tastes form a worldwide confederacy and communicate by means of an esoteric code unknown to people with heterosexual tastes is simply a piece of sexual mythology.

It is, however, a piece of mythology which fits very well into the overall aesthetic philosophy of *A la recherche*, and this is no doubt one reason Proust preserves it.

Notes

45. For further thoughts on this idea see Tripp, pp. 67–68.

46. *Great Dialogues of Plato*, pp. 133–34; *A la recherche*, 2: 614 ff., especially 623–26.

47. Symonds in Cory, p. 4.

48. Quoted and translated by Symonds in Cory, p. 19.

49. Symonds in Cory, p. 19; Tarnowsky, tr. Gardner, p. 120; and Paolo Mantegazza, "The Perversions of Love," in Cory, p. 259.

50. Richard Burton, "Terminal Essay: *The Book of the Thousand Nights and a Night*," in Cory, p. 218; Edward Carpenter, "The Intermediate Sex," in Cory, p. 155.

51. Quoted and translated in Richard Lewinsohn, *A History of Sexual Customs*, tr. Alexander Mayce, p. 342.

52. George Weinberg, p. 64.

53. Quoted and translated in Steakley, p. 82.

—J. E. Rivers, *Proust and the Art of Love*, (New York: Columbia University Press, 1980): 168-172.

Elyane Dezon-Jones on the Significance of the Grandmother

[Elyane Dezon-Jones is Professor of French at Washington University, author of *Proust et L'Amerique*, and a Chevalier of the Ordre des Palmes Académique. In this section, she develops the often-overlooked importance of the role played by Marcel's grandmother.]

It seems that up till now Proust critics have rather neglected studying the genesis and the function of the figure of the grandmother in *A la recherche du temps perdu*, when in fact she takes her place at the point of departure and of arrival of the narrator's literary vocation. She initiates him to aestheticism in *Du côté de chez Swann* ("instead of photographs of Chartres Cathedral, of the Fountains of Saint-Cloud, or of Vesuvius, she would inquire of Swann whether some great painter had not depicted them, and preferred to give me photographs of "Chartres Cathedral" after Corot, of the "Fountains of Saint-Cloud" after Hubert Robert, and of "Vesuvius" after Turner, which were a stage higher in the scale of art") (*RTP* 1:40; *RTPK* 1:43); in *A l'ombre des jeunes filles en fleurs*, she lets him benefit by her connections when she gives him an entrée into "society" by introducing the narrator to Mme. de Villeparisis; she dies in *Le Côté de Guermantes* the better to reappear in *Sodome et Gomorrhe* under the form of an intermittency of the heart, becoming the epicentre of the Proustian approach to seeking a praxis of the "combined forces of memory and imagination."

The grandmother is a character very different from the others from many points of view but chiefly because her function consists of dying that the text may live. It was therefore necessary for Proust to make her stand out in a radical way. He did so by setting her aside from the original group (the family cell), which explains the numerous references to the grandmother's "eccentricities" in *Du côté de chez Swann*, and beyond the reference group (the Guermantes) by presenting her as the constant modifying factor in the narrator's point of view. She had to die—stop incarnating a, world where appearances are not misleading—so that the narrator could name the false appearances by their true names.

When he goes to the theater to see la Berma for the first time, the narrator appeals to his grandmother to straighten out the confusion which is inherent to his vision of the world: "I told my grandmother that I could not see very well and she handed me her glasses" (*RTP* 1:449; *RTPK* 1:484). This act will be repeated by the narrator become novelist at the end of *Le Temps retrouvé* when he offers his reader his book as an optical instrument enabling him to see reality more exactly. So the grandmother is the indispensable intermediary who potentializes the focus of the whole work and the clarification of the role of the creative artist. She appears and disappears at strategic moments of the fictional life of the narrator to organize the stages which will lead to the recognition of "the invisible vocation of which this book is the history" (*RTP* 2:397; *RTPK* 2:412).

If she sometimes gives the impression of being a minor character, a convenient marionette, a slightly ridiculous old woman, a mere accompanist, a duplicate of the mother, a fanatical reader of Mme. de Sévigné, an "imbecile," it is because she will be embodied in the narrative only after her death. Before that there will only be brief snatches of a partly glimpsed individual. It is in order to reconstitute this character that the work will be composed. All we see of the grandmother, up till the day of her death, is a cheek that the child kisses and a pair of arms which she protectively folds around him. Her face is never described in its totality but only in terms of the emotions that modify her gaze, the expression of her mouth, and the wrinkles on her forehead. As for her voice, we only hear "fragments" of it.

The grandmother is in a perpetual process of modification even when she is supposed to represent that stabilizing influence in the narrator's life. She is reduced to a simple "face" when Proust depicts the physical sufferings to which her illness subjects her: "her face, worn, diminished, terrifyingly expressive, seemed like the rude, flushed, purplish, desperate face of some wild guardian of a tomb in a primitive, almost prehistoric sculpture" (*RTP* 2:324; *RTPK* 2:335). The grandmother is truly the "guardian of the tomb" constituted by the book which is still to be written. In fact, when Professor E ... announces to the narrator "Your grandmother is doomed" ("Votre grandmère est perdue"), he states a condition without which the thematics of *A la recherche du temps perdu* could not function. In order to recover his grandmother, which is as much as to say recompose her eternal body, it only remains to the narrator to undo the work of time, by substituting life for death: "Life in withdrawing from her had taken with it the disillusionments of life. A smile seemed to be hovering on my grandmother's lips. On that funeral couch, death, like a sculptor of the Middle Ages, had laid her down in the form of a young girl" (*RTP* 2:345; *RTPK* 2:357).

It really is a question, for the narrator, of *setting down on paper* the body of the grandmother "in the form of a young girl" so satisfying his ambition to isolate "a fragment of time in the pure state" (*RTP* 3:872; *RTPK* 3:905). She goes from being a guardian of the tomb to becoming the goal of the quest. From being a face, she becomes the body of the narrative. She is an avatar of the "mighty goddess of Time" (*RTP* 3:387; *RTPK* 3:393) which the narrator will believe he sees in the sleeping Albertine *laid* (*or set down*) on her bed.

In a dream, the narrator repeats the voyage of Orpheus, the oneiric journey which is to snatch the grandmother back from oblivion.

> ... as soon as, to traverse the arteries of the subterranean city, we have embarked upon the dark current of our own blood as upon an inward Lethe meandering sixfold, tall solemn forms appear to us, approach and glide away, leaving us in tears. I sought in vain for my grandmother's form when I had entered beneath the somber portals; yet I knew that she did exist still, if with a diminished vitality, as pale as that of memory; the darkness was increasing, and the wind; my father who was to take me to her, had not yet arrived. Suddenly my breath failed me, I felt my heart turn to stone; I had just remembered that for weeks on end I had forgotten to write to my grandmother. (RTP 2:760; RTPK 2:787–88)

This passage makes it clear that the narrator is in search of the divine afflatus. The grandmother's disappearance is bound up with failure to write. She will only be brought back to the land of the living by the achievement of the literary work whose inspiration she is in every sense of the word:

> "Where is grandmother? Tell me her address. Is she all right? Are you quite sure she has everything she needs? "Yes, yes," says my father, "you needn't worry. Her nurse is well trained. We send her a little money from time to time, so that she can get your grandmother anything she may need. She sometimes asks what's become of you. She was told you were going to write a book. She seemed pleased. She wiped away a tear" (RTP 2:761; RTPK 2:788)

In search of the lost grandmother, the narrator will once more attempt "the desperate stratagem of a condemned prisoner" (*RTP* 1:28; *RTPK* 1:30), the same stratagem he had used to get his mother to come to him in the initial scene of Combray, to cancel her absence, to erase the time spent without her: that is by writing, no longer a brief and clumsy note, but three thousand pages organized to form a work of art. Thus he will guarantee eternity to the character of the grandmother, who becomes a determining creation, leading to the fundamental difference between the disorganization of *Jean Santeuil*, from which she is absent and from which a real standard of objective validity is absent in consequence, and the coherence of *A la recherche du temps perdu* for which she provides a structure. It is in fact the grandmother who becomes the focal point for the existential anguish of separation which the narrator will soothe *by recounting it*. This is what puts the scene of the mother's goodnight kiss in its proper perspective: the temporary absence of the mother is only the "rehearsal" of the permanent absence of the grandmother. The "drame du coucher" (bedtime drama) is nothing more than the pale prefiguration of the tragedy which the death of his grandmother—any death—will constitute for the narrator. "There is no reply" to the note sent by Marcel to his mother, for their separation is not permanent. In contrast, the only possible reply to the death of the grandmother is the act of writing which will bring her back to life, showing how true it is that "real life, life at last laid bare and illuminated—the only life in consequence which can be said to be really lived—is literature" (*RTP* 3:895; *RTPK* 3:931).

Note

*This essay was written specifically for this volume and is published here for the first time by permission of the author. Translated by the editor, with the exception of the quotations from *A la recherche du temps perdu*, which have been taken from the Kilmartin translation.

—Elyane Dezon-Jones, from *Critical Essays on Marcel Proust* (edited by Barbara J. Bucknall, Boston: G. K. Hall, 1987): 192-195.

Barbara J. Bucknall on "Gomorrah"

[Barbara Bucknall taught in both the United States and Canada, serving in the French department at Brock University. She is also the author of *The Religion of Art in Proust*. Here she follows as Proust turns his attention from the descendents of "Sodom" (male homosexuals) to those of "Gomorrah" (lesbians).]

In this chapter, to use Proust's terminology, Gomorrah joins Sodom. But not immediately, because the narrator continues to trace the line of his fading grief and shows how he begins to hope for happiness with Albertine and even to desire her, although he tries to distract this desire for a while by gazing at the sea. Finally he sets off in search of Albertine. But once he is in the local train he has an involuntary memory of his grandmother and of the distress she had felt when he got slightly drunk in the train from Paris to Balbec on their previous visit. He gets off the train and walks back to Balbec, admiring the hawthorns as he goes. As soon as he gets back to the hotel, he sends Françoise to fetch Albertine. He is a little anxious over the time she takes to come, but when she arrives she appears to be all willingness to answer his beck and call. Françoise, however, announces that Albertine will only cause him grief, a prediction that is all too true.

The Princesse de Parme appears in the dining room of the Grand Hotel. For a moment the narrator takes pleasure in observing her. But he is chiefly preoccupied with girls, and he informs us that he took his pleasure with 13 of Albertine's friends during this stay at Balbec, quite as much as with Albertine, although he wanted Albertine from time to time. He has no suspicions to arouse his anxious doubts where she is concerned until Dr. Cottard, one day at the Casino of Incarville, watching Andrée and Albertine dancing together, remarks that their breasts are touching and they must be reaching orgasm.

It takes a while for the suffering this remark causes the narrator to sink in. At the same time he is gradually becoming attached to Albertine because of the excuses she makes to avoid seeing him whenever he wants. (It is a Proustian axiom noticed before that people always want to see those people who show that they are not particularly keen on seeing them.) When Albertine sees the narrator, she appears excited by his presence, but this does not jibe with her eagerness to go and see someone else. The narrator's questions about the other person she has to go and see are already beginning to take on the inquisitorial tone of the questions he is to ask later on, when it will be a matter of life and death to him to find out what she is concealing from him—particularly her lesbianism. In fact, it is not long before the name of Sappho enters the discussion, even on this relatively peaceful occasion.

A few days later the narrator will be in the Casino of Balbec with Andrée and Albertine when Bloch's sister and a girl cousin come in and make an exhibition of their lesbianism. The cousin is well known at Balbec for having an affair with an actress. Andrée expresses virtuous indignation, and she and Albertine turn their backs on the guilty pair, but Albertine lets slip that she had been watching them in a mirror all the time they were there.

Albertine's actions would seem to confirm Cottard's opinion of her lesbianism, but oddly enough the narrator claims not to share it. When he joins Andrée at Elstir's house, he is so impressed by her poise and dignity that he cannot believe she is a lesbian—at any rate for the moment. These suspicions come and go, as he remembers what he has been told of Mme Swann, and he mentally notes that he is glad that he is not in love with Albertine. He demonstrates to himself and Albertine that he is not in love with her by addressing offensive remarks to her the next time he sees her while being extremely pleasant to Andrée.

At this point the Cambremers turn up, and the narrator's mother seeks refuge inside the hotel. There is a very comic description of the way in which the dowager Marquise de Cambremer has adorned herself to be worthy of her social duties. Her daughter-in-law is all smiles because she has heard from Robert de Saint-Loup that the narrator is on close terms with the Guermantes family. The narrator remarks that this is the descent of the Cambremers that his grandmother had been afraid of, but notes that it had happened quite differently from the way she had expected. This episode in itself is hardly worth mentioning, except that it is an illustration of the Proustian axiom that certain events that do not at first seem possible to the objective observer do in fact come to pass, but in quite different ways than one would have expected. In fact this axiom has been true of the narrator's whole dealings with the Guermantes family, not to mention Gilberte and Bergotte, but it suits Proust's sense of humor to underline it, at this point, with reference to the Cambremers.

The conversation between the narrator, the dowager Marquise de Cambremer, the young Marquise de Cambremer, and their guest, a lawyer, is highly entertaining. The dowager Marquise has a true appreciation of the arts but which makes her drool, the young Marquise is a fervent defender of the avant-garde but has no real appreciation of anything that is not fashionable, the lawyer has the bad taste to admire Le Sidaner, and the narrator has the advantage of calmly understanding what he admires while coolly toppling the young Marquise's prejudices. Albertine is present but has very little to say. Presumably she is admiring the narrator's self-assurance—that is, if her mind is not on something else. At any rate, she has nothing to say when the young Marquise and the lawyer criticize Elstir, whom she knows and admires. But then, as a *jeune fille*, she is not supposed to push herself forward. She only opens up a little when she has an opportunity to talk about the seagulls, which remind her of Amsterdam; she leaves it to her boyfriend to be an arbiter in matters of taste. In fact, he gives the reader the benefit of his considered views on changes in artistic fashions rather than lecturing his immediate audience. However, out of the kindness of his heart, he does tell the young Marquise that Debussy admires Chopin, for she had always despised her mother-in-law for her devotion to Chopin.

This select company having departed, the narrator takes Albertine up to his room. This man who hates being lied to is a very skillful liar himself, as Howard Moss observes.[3] When Albertine asks him what he has against her, he proceeds to spin a long tale about how he is in love with Andrée and has come to resent Albertine because he has been told that she had sexual relations with Andrée. He obtains a spirited denial from

Albertine, and then feels free to be affectionate with her. At the same time, he has obtained from Albertine a refusal to leave him in order to go and have dinner with her aunt. Thus he has succeeded in dominating her more completely than ever before—a need for dominance being one of the salient characteristics of what Proust calls love. In the narrator's opinion he should have left Albertine then and lived with the memory of what had at least seemed to be the love that he had succeeded in inspiring, for he is not a being for whom reciprocal love is possible.

Given the narrator's temperament, it is not surprising that his actual reaction to this high point in their relationship, if it is not to avoid Albertine completely, is to spend more time with his mother, who reminisces to him about his grandmother and their days in Combray. In order to revive his memory of their painted plates illustrating the *Arabian Nights*, his mother, at his request, orders for him the two French translations of the *Arabian Nights*, by Galland and Mardrus, but is shocked by the obscenity of the latter. This little episode has more importance than one might think, for in *Le Temps retrouvé* the narrator speaks of writing a new *Arabian Nights*.

However, the narrator does manage to have solitary strolls with Albertine, in between getting the Dutch courage to issue invitations to other girls he fancies. But as more girls arrive at Balbec, the more afraid he becomes that Albertine is going to take an interest in one of them. He is particularly worried that Mme de Putbus's chambermaid, whom he had not so long ago wanted for himself, will join forces with Albertine, to the point where he would like to get that chambermaid dismissed. Meanwhile Albertine and Andrée are very careful to dispel the narrator's doubts about them.

Around this time, Bloch's sister makes love with a former actress in the dance hall, causing a scandal that, however, has no unpleasant consequences for them, because M. Nissim Bernard, Bloch's uncle, who is homosexual himself, is able to pull strings for them. It is interesting to see how the novel's tone changes from one of anxiety and alarm to that of tolerant amusement as soon as we pass from female to male homosexuality. But we pass again from this topic to a conversation between the narrator and Marie Gineste and Céleste Albaret, two sisters whom Proust knew in real life, for no apparent reason but for the fun of it. Then we come back to the shameless lesbian pair whom Bloch ignores in the street while the narrator expresses his fears that their indecent utterances are addressed to Albertine.

NOTE

3. Howard Moss, *The Magic Lantern of Marcel Proust* (London: Faber and Faber, 1963), 52; hereafter cited in text.

—Barbara J. Bucknall, *Marcel Proust Revisited*, (New York: Twayne Publishers, 1992): 73-77.

INGRID WASSENAAR ON PARTIES AND SELF-JUSTIFICATION

[Ingrid Wassenaar is a Fellow of Christ's College at Cambridge University, specializing in literary criticism and twentieth-century French literature, and the author of *Marcel Proust: A Beginner's Guide*. In this extract, she discusses the reception given by the Princesse de Guermantes, and specifically the disclosure of Swann's moribund condition.]

This question of an appeal reminds us of Legrandin's *bête immonde*, and Mme de Marsantes's *empressement*, of Swann's *muflerie intermittente* and Marcel's *purs mots de conversation*; and it redirects our attention to the underground grumbling of our original curiosity about why the narrator goes to so many parties and describes them at such length. The narrator is concerned at all times with small talk which gives away a great deal of information, manipulating it in order to disguise his own vulnerabilities, and astonished when he hears moments of vulnerability break through the indifferent veneer offered by others. He learns to imitate indifference as a self-preservative form of justification that allows him to fit into a hostile social group. But one final experiment in the public functioning of self-justification remains, and it takes place at the apogee of the series of Faubourg Saint-Germain parties, a *soirée* held by the princesse de Guermantes. The account of the party circles around Swann, his mortal illness, and the mysterious conversation he has had with the anti-dreyfusard prince de Guermantes. When Marcel sees Swann, ambiguous reactions result (. . .)

The *tristesse* about Swann's impending death that the narrator thinks no one else feels is not so far from their *fascination*. It had been the narrator, not Saint-Loup, who had quoted from Lucretius, but again attributing it to somebody else: when the duc de Guermantes had complained about Bornier's play, *La Fille de Roland*, the narrator's use of the quotation had referred to the duc's complacency, 'par le *suave mari magno* que nous éprouvons, au milieu d'un bon dîner, à nous souvenir d'aussi terribles soirées' (ii. 780; tr. iii. 566).[34] Projecting complacency and prurient attention onto other onlookers shields the narrator from admitting to its manifestation in himself. But later, he cannot resist focusing on Swann's marked skin: 'Sa figure se marquait de petits points bleu de Prusse, qui avaient l'air de ne pas appartenir an monde vivant, et dégageait ce genre d'odeur qui, au lycée, après les "expériences", rend si désagréable de rester dans une classe de "Sciences"' (iii. 98; tr. iv. 115). Having set up distaste about Swann's physical degeneration as other people's negative judgement, the narrator can himself enjoy chemicalizing the illness and drawing an analogy with a scientific experiment. Marcel's specular relation to Swann is that of fascinated revulsion. The aural relation postponed throughout the party is an account of Swann's conversation with the prince de Guermantes, which takes the form of a confession. Swann's intimate confession has also effectively been postponed throughout the novel, and the pressure of its delay increases its cathartic potential to extreme proportions. (. . .)

His words are an attempt to justify by reconciliation various factors in his life, and they constitute a warning to the young narrator. Swann implies that he did not even benefit from the advantages of jealousy, 'par la faute de ma nature qui n'est pas capable de réflexions trés prolongées' and 'par la faute de la femme, je veux dire des femmes, dont j'ai été jaloux' (iii. 101; tr. iv. 119). Here telling the truth masks an appeal for sympathetic reassurance. But his self-castigation really is a truth about himself, and not an exaggeration needing a corrective reassurance. The honesty of his truth-telling is called into question by his parapraxis immediately afterwards: for the depth of his jealousy extended only to *one* rather than to *many* women. His mistake demonstrates his sense that jealousy might be worthwhile if multiply experienced. Jealousy over just one, rather worthless, woman, however, is not good enough. His Don Juanism stops short at 'dont j'ai ... '. He attempts self-critique: 'Même quand on ne tient plus aux choses, il n'est pas absolument indifférent d'y avoir tenu, parce que c'était toujours pour des raisons qui échappaient aux autres. Le souvenir de ces sentiments-là, nous sentons qu'il n'est qu'en nous; c'est en nous qu'il faut rentrer pour le regarder' (iii. 101; tr. iv. 119).

While the conclusions are no different from those that the narrator will eventually formulate and turn into laws of the self, Swann misjudges and plays down his own discovery, calling his maxim-making a 'jargon idéaliste' (iii. 101; tr. iv. 119). Having misjudged, in Proustian terms, his own best attempt to formulate a law of the self, he withdraws from a universal statement to his personal experience, hoping it will speak for itself, but deliberately articulating it as understatement: 'ce que je veux dire, c'est que j'ai beaucoup aimé la vie et que j'ai beaucoup aimé les arts' (iii. 101; tr. iv. 119). He tries to raise love to the status of sole criterion of importance in life, but he gives away the emptiness of his words: 'maintenant que je suis un peu trop fatigué pour vivre avec les autres, ces anciens sentiments si personnels à moi que j'ai eus, me semblent, *ce qui est la manie de tous les collectionneurs*, trés précieux' (iii. 101–2; tr. iv. 119; my emphasis). By identifying himself as a collector, Swann's words point up the devastating effects that indifference has had. Instead of investing himself in love as he says he has done, he has invested himself in investment, because the safer risk of collecting up *anciens sentiments*, instead of acquiescing in the instability and fragility of emotions, has allowed him to maintain an indifferent control over those feelings. Swann's self-appraisal is an arthritic articulation, since his past and present are mentioned in the span of a single sentence, but are no longer of any use to him. We have, of course, seen his elegant talent for division, which actually spells out useless confusion, in other parts of the novel. Compare this passage from *Un amour de Swann*, in which he is neatly distinguishing between the functions of the artist and the critic (. . .)

The formal perfection of the binary rhetorical structure at the end, each half divided into three parts, is designed to seem coherent, flowing from an immanent logic of what artists and collectors are. It is the third term of each half of the pair which attracts attention. The third term in a classic triple construction emphasizes and summarizes the preceding items. *Désintéressement* and *sensualité*, however, do not form natural compounds with their intended partners. They are only attached to their respective sides of the equation by force of rhetoric, and could just as easily be transposed. Each term thus undermines the triple in which it has been located, *désintéressement* by its potentially negative connotation of a detachment that amounts to cold indifference, *sensualité* by the connotation it has of being proper to the senses, and therefore a vital attribute for an artist, as well as simply applicable to someone who seeks gratification of the senses. *Désintéressement*, furthermore, signifies both disinterestedness and the reparation of a debt. The uneasy suspension and separation of the triples into an apparent binary opposition works against Swann. Rather than generating a satisfactory poignancy, in which his thwarted status as artist is set off by an ironic identification with something less valuable (the status of collector), the opposition constantly threatens to collapse. Misjudgement is marked by the violation of a rhetorical structure.

Un amour de Swann, however, relies on the illusion of completion and distance afforded by its third-person voice. It is far more disconcerting to feel the urgency and compression of Swann's first-person speech, injected right into the ambit of another's first-person sampling of party-prattle, as the dying man reports the content of a conversation he has just had with the prince de Guermantes. Swann performs it, even introducing another character, the abbé Poiré. The following quotation, which is practically impossible to represent within the conventions of English typography, demonstrates graphically how too many voices spoil the plot. Swann is here speaking to the narrator, but *quoting* the prince de Guermantes, *in the act of quoting l'abbé*: ' " ' "Non," me répondit l'abbé,' (je vous dis *me*," me dit Swann, "parce que c'est le prince qui me parle, vous comprenez?)"' (iii. 109; tr. iv. 128).

The story narrates the previously staunchly anti-dreyfusard prince's realization of Dreyfus's innocence and the army's corruption. In his eagerness to relate this *palinodie*, this retraction, to the narrator, and to maximize its dramatic effect, Swann selects the mode of direct speech, reporting a conversation which reports another conversation, each retold as though in present time. The effect of this is to implicate Swann completely in a particularly complex process of narration. His own illness and impending death are displaced: 'Seulement, j'avoue que ce serait bien agaçant de mourir avant la fin de l'affaire Dreyfus' (iii. 112; tr. iv. 131). Displacing his own mortality into another apparently unrelated issue, itself indifferent to his interest in it, is simultaneously objective and ridiculous. He is adopting the indifference shown by the Guermantes towards the idea of his death as his own attitude. Appropriating a political event as a substitute for his own importance in the world is as empty of significance as ignoring the world to concentrate on a round of parties.

Indifference has ruined Swann's life, and here is his deathbed account of it, presented to the narrator, who has sought out Swann with determination to hear it. Yet the narrator fails to respond. He does not allow the dying man the credit of his report: 'Swann oubliait que dans l'après-midi, il m'avait dit au contraire que les opinions en cette affaire Dreyfus étaient commandées par l'atavisme. Tout au plus avait-il fait exception pour l'intelligence ... C'était donc maintenant à la droiture du coeur qu'il donnait le rôle dévolu tantôt a l'intelligence' (iii. 110; tr. iv. 129). The narrator's critical appraisal of Swann's political integrity shows no mercy, and no interest in Swann's motivation.

It is as though the indifference displayed by the people who currently surround the narrator has been imported as a ready-made solution to a difficult encounter: like Swann, the narrator is also imitating the Guermantes. Swann's indifference to his own life means that he cannot draw conclusions about it, but only have it conclude, while the narrator's artificially imported indifference to the promptings of his self-justificatory consciousness leave him deaf to the potential for judgement about his own future actions that Swann offers.

Note

34. 'Suave, mari magno turbantibus aequora ventis, I e terra magnum alterius spectare laborem' (Pleasant it is, when over a great sea the winds trouble the waters, to gaze from shore upon another's great tribulation), Lucretius, *De rerum natura*, 2, 1–2.

—Ingrid Wassenaar, Proustian Passions: *The Uses of Self-Justification for A la recherche du temps perdu*, (Oxford: Oxford University Press, 2000): 66-71.

WORKS BY

Marcel Proust

Les Plaisirs et les jours. 1896.
Pleasures and Regrets (translated by Louise Varese). 1948.
Pleasures and Days, and Other Writings (translated by Barbara Dupee, Gerard Hopkins, and Louise Varese). 1957.

Du côté de chez Swann. 1913.
Swann's Way (translated by C. K. Scott Moncrieff). 1922.

Pastiches et mélanges. 1919.

preface to *Propos de peintre: De David à Degas* (by Jacques-Emile Blanche). 1919.

A l'ombre des jeunes filles en fleurs. 1919.
Within a Budding Grove (translated by C. K. Scott Moncrieff). 1924.

Le Côté de Guermantes I. 1920.
The Guermantes Way (translated by C. K. Scott Moncrieff). 1925.

Le Côté de Guermantes II – Sodome et Gomorrhe I. 1921.
Le Côté de Guermantes II included in *The Guermantes Way* (translated by C. K. Scott Moncrieff). 1925.
Cities of the Plain (translated by C. K. Scott Moncrieff). 1927.

Sodome et Gomorrhe II. 1922.
included in *Cities of the Plain* (translated by C. K. Scott Moncrieff). 1927.

Sodome et Gomorrhe III: La Prisonnière. 1923.
The Captive (translated by C. K. Scott Moncrieff). 1929.

Albertine disparue. 1925.
The Sweet Cheat Gone (translated by C. K. Scott Moncrieff). 1930.

Le Temps retrouvé. 1927.
The Past Recaptured (translated by Frederick A. Blossom). 1932.

Chroniques. 1927.

Le Balzac de Monsieur de Guermantes. 1950.

Jean Santeuil. 1952.
Jean Santeuil (translated by Gerard Hopkins). 1955.

A la recherche du temps perdu (Pléiade edition). 1954.

Contre Sainte-Beuve, suivi de Nouveaux Mélanges. 1954.
On Art and Literature 1896-1919 (translated by Sylvia Townsend). 1958.

Textes retrouvés (edited by Philip Kolb and Larkin Price). 1968.

Les Pastiches de Proust (edited by Jean Milly). 1970.

Le Carnet de 1908 (edited by Philip Kolb). 1976.

L'Indifférent. 1978.

Matinée chez la princesse de Guermantes (edited by Henri Bonnet and Bernard Brun). 1982.

Poèmes (edited by Claude Francis and Fernande Gontier). 1982.

TRANSLATIONS

French translation of *The Bible of Amiens* (by John Ruskin) as *La Bible d'Amiens*. 1904.

French translation of *Sesame and Lilies* (by John Ruskin) as *Sésame et les lys: Des trésors des rois*. 1906.

LETTERS

Comment debut a Marcel Proust: Lettres inedites. Nouvelle Revue Francais, 1925.

Lettres inedites. Bangeres-de-Bigorre, 1926.

Correspondance générale de Marcel Proust (edited by Paul Brach, Robert Proust, and Suzy Proust-Mante). 1930-1936.

Letters of Marcel Proust (edited and translated by Mina Curtiss). 1949.

Forty-seven Unpublished Letters From Marcel Proust to Walter Berry (edited and translated by Caresse and Henry Crosby). 1930.

Letters a la N.R.F. 1932.

Lettres a un ami, recueil de quarante-et-une lettres inedites addresses a Marie Nordlinger, 1889-1908. 1942.

Lettres á Madame C. 1946.

Letters of Marcel Proust (edited and translated by Mina Curtiss). 1948.

Lettres á André Gide. 1949.

Letters de Marcel Proust á Bibesco. 1949

Marcel Proust: Correspondance avec sa mère (edited by Philip Kolb). 1953.

Marcel Proust: Letters to His Mother (edited and translated by George Painter). 1956.

Lettres á Reynaldo Hahn. 1956.

Correspondance de Marcel Proust (edited by Philip Kolb). 1970-.

Selected Letters, 1880-1903 (edited by Philip Kolb, translated by Ralph Mannheim). 1983.

WORKS ABOUT

Marcel Proust

Albaret, Céleste. *Monsieur Proust* (as told to Georges Belmont). Paris: Laffont, 1973.

———. *Monsieur Proust* (translated by Barbara Bray). London: Collins, Harvill Press, 1976.

Alden, Douglas. *Marcel Proust and His French Critics*. Los Angeles: Lymanhouse, 1940.

Ames, Van Meter. *Proust and Santayana: The Aesthetic Way of Life*. New York: Russell & Russell, 1964.

Barker, Richard. *Marcel Proust*. New York: Criterion Press, 1958.

Bell, Clive. *Proust*. New York: Hogarth Press, 1928.

Bloom, Harold. *Marcel Proust*. Philadelphia: Chelsea House Publishers, 1987.

Brée, Germaine. *The World of Marcel Proust*. Boston: Houghton Mifflin, 1966.

Cahiers Marcel Proust. Paris: Gallimard, 1927-1935. New series, 1970-.

Chefdor, Monique (editor). *In Search of Marcel Proust*. Claremont: Scripps College and the Ward Ritchie Press, 1973.

Clarac, Pierre, and Ferré, André. *Album Proust*. Paris: Gallimard, 1965.

Coleman, Elliott. *The Golden Angel: Papers on Proust*. New York: Coley Taylor, 1954.

Contemporary Authors, volume 120. Detroit: Gale Research, 1987.

Deleuze, Gilles. *Marcel Proust et les signes*. Paris: Presses Universitaires de France, 1964.

———. *Proust and Signs* (translated by Richard Howard). New York: Braziller, 1972.

The Dictionary of Literary Biography, volume 65: French Novelists 1900-1930. Detroit: Gale Research, 1988.

Doubrovsky, Serge. *La Place de la madeleine*. Paris: Mercure de France, 1974.

———. *Writing and Fantasy in Proust* (translated by Carol Mastrangelo Bové and Paul Bové). Lincoln & London: University of Nebraska Press, 1986.

Ellis, Havelock. *From Rousseau to Proust*. Cambridge: Riverside Press, 1935.

Forster, E. M. *Abinger Harvest*. New York: Harcourt Brace Jovanovich, Inc., 1936.

Girard, René, editor. *Proust: A Collection of Critical Essays*. Englewood Cliffs: Prentice-Hall, 1962.

Graham, Victor. *The Imagery of Proust*. Oxford: Blackwell, 1966.

Haldane, Charlotte. *Marcel Proust*. London: Arthur Baker, 1951.

Hindus, Milton. *The Proustian Vision*. New York: Columbia University Press, 1954.

———. *A Reader's Guide to Marcel Proust*. New York: Noonday Press, 1962.

Hughes, Edward. *Marcel Proust: A Study in the Quality of Awareness*. Cambridge: Cambridge University Press, 1983.

Kawin, Bruce. *The Mind of the Novel: Reflexive Fiction and theIneffable*. Princeton: Princeton University Press, 1982.

Kazin, Alfred. *The Inmost Leaf: A Selection of Essays*. New York: Harcourt, 1955.

Kilmartin, Terence. *A Reader's Guide to "Remembrance of Things Past"*. New York: Random House, 1983.

———. "*Translating Proust.*" Grand Street I, number 1 (Autumn, 1981): pages 134-46.

Kopp, Richard. *Marcel Proust As a Social Critic*. Rutherford: Fairleigh Dickinson University Press, 1971.

Lemaitre, Georges. *Four French Novelists: Marcel Proust, André Gide, Jean Giraudoux, Paul Morand*. Port Washington: Kennikat Press, 1969.

Leon, Derrick. *Introduction to Proust: His Life, His Circle, His Work*. London: Kegan Paul, 1940.

Lesage, Laurent. *Marcel Proust and His Literary Friends*. Urbana: University of Illinois Press, 1958.

Levin, Harry. *The Gates of Horn: A Study of Five French Realists*. New York: Oxford University Press, 1963.

Linder, Gladys Dudley (editor). *Marcel Proust: Reviews and Estimates*. Stanford: Stanford University Press, 1942.

March, Harold. *The Two Worlds of Marcel Proust*. Philadelphia: University of Pennsylvania Press, 1948.

Maurois, André. *A la recherche de Marcel Proust*. Paris: Hachette, 1949.

———. *The Quest for Proust* (translated by Gerard Hopkins). London, Cape, 1950. (US title: *Proust, Portrait of a Genius*. New York: Harper, 1950.)

May, Derwent. *Proust*. New York: Oxford University Press, 1983.

Moss, Howard. *The Magic Lantern of Marcel Proust*. New York: Macmillan, 1962.

Peyre, Henri. *Marcel Proust*. Columbia Essays on Modern Writers Pamphelet number 48. New York: Columbia University Press, 1970.

Price, Larkin. *Marcel Proust: A Critical Panorama*. Urbana: University of Illinois Press, 1973.

Quennel, Peter (editor). *Marcel Proust, 1871-1922: A Centenary Volume*. London: Weidenfeld and Nicolson, 1971.

Rawlinson, Mary. *"Art and Truth: Reading Proust."* Philosophy and Literature 6, numbers 1-2 (October 1982): pages 1-16.

———. *"Proust's Impressionism."* L'Esprit Créateur XXIV, number 2 (Summer, 1984): pages 80-91.

Rogers, Brian. *Proust's Narrative Techniques*. Geneva: Droz, 1965.

Sansom, William. *Proust and His World*. London: Thames & Hudson, 1973.

Spalding, P. A. *A Reader's Handbook to Proust: An Index Guide to "Remembrance of Things Past."* New York: Barnes & Noble, 1975.

Steel, Gareth. *Chronology and Time in "A la recherche du temps perdu."* Geneva: Droz, 1979.

Strauss, Walter. *Proust and Literature: The Novelist as Critic.* Cambridge: Harvard University Press, 1957.

Tadié, Jean-Yves. *Marcel Proust*. New York: Viking, 2001.

Taylor, Elizabeth Russell. *Marcel Proust and His Contexts: A Bibliography of English-Language Scholarship*. New York & London: Garland, 1981.

Twentieth-Century Literary Criticism volume 7; volume 13; volume 33. Detroit: Gale Research, 1982, 1984, 1989.

Vogely, Maxine Arnold. *A Proust Dictionary*. Troy, New York: The Whitston Publishing Company, 1981.

ACKNOWLEDGMENTS

Excerpts from *Illuminations* by Walter Benjamin. © 1968 by Walter Benjamin. Reprinted by permission of Harcourt, Inc.

Proust by Samuel Beckett: pp. 2-7. © 1931 by Grove Press. Reprinted by permission.

Brée, Germaine, *Marcel Proust and Deliverance from Time*. © 1955 by the trustees of Rutgers College in New Jersey and © 1969 by Rutgers University. Reprinted by permission of Rutgers University Press.

Proust's Nocturnal Muse by William Stewart Bell: pp. 112-115. © 1962 by Columbia University Press. Reprinted by permission.

On Proust by Jean-François Revel: pp. 93-100. Reprinted by permission of Open Court Publishing Company, a division of Caras Publishing Company, Peru, IL, from *On Proust* by Jean-François Revel, © 1972 by The Library Press.

Reprinted from Gérard Genette, *Narrative Discourse Revisited*. Translated from the French by Jane E. Lewin. © 1980 by Cornell University Press. Used by permission of the publisher, Cornell University Press.

Marcel Proust—An English Tribute by J. Middleton Murry: pp. 106-110. © 1923 by Thomas Seltzer. Reprinted by permission.

Nostalgia: A Psychoanalytic Study of Marcel Proust by Milton L. Miller: pp. 28-31. © 1954 by Milton L Miller. Reprinted by permission of Houghton Mifflin Company. All rights reserved.

Proust's Way: An Essay in Descriptive Criticism by Georges Piroué: pp. 41-44. © 1957 by William Heinemann Ltd. Reprinted by permission.

A Reading of Proust by Wallace Fowlie: pp. 67-72. © 1964 by Wallace Fowlie. Used by permission of Doubleday, a division of Random House, Inc.

Marcel Proust: A Guide to the Main Recurrent Themes by Raymond T. Riva: pp. 195-200. © 1965 by Raymond T. Riva. Reprinted by permission.

The Proustian Community by Seth L. Wolitz: pp. 51-53. © 1971 by New York University Press. Reprinted by permission.

Poulet, Georges. Translated by Elliott Colman. *Proustian Space*: pp. 7-13. © 1977 by Georges Poulet. Reprinted by permission of The Johns Hopkins University Press.

Excerpts from *Lectures on Literature* by Vladimir Nabokov: © 1980 by the Estate of Vladimir Nabokov. Reprinted by permission of Harcourt, Inc.

Proust: Collected Essays on the Writer and His Art by J. M. Cocking: pp. 53-55. © 1982 by Cambridge University Press. Reprinted by permission of Cambridge University Press.

Marcel Proust by Philip Thody: pp. 36-39. © 1988 by St. Martin's Press. Reprinted by permission.

Marcel Proust: His Life and Work by Léon Pierre-Quint: pp. 195-200. © 1927 by Alfred A. Knopf. Reprinted by permission.

The Mind of Proust by Frederick Charles Green: pp. 197-200. © 1949 by Cambridge University Press. Reprinted by permission of Cambridge University Press.

Marcel Proust, The Fictions of Life and Art by Leo Bersani: pp. 63-65. © 1965 by Oxford University Press. Reprinted by permission.

Marcel Proust by Roger Shattuck: pp. 58-65. © 1974 by Princeton University Press. Reprinted by permission.

Marcel Proust by Patrick Brady: pp. 26-30. © 1977 by Twayne Publishers. Reprinted by permission of the Gale Group.

The Proustian Comedy by Jack Murray: pp. 88-92. © 1980 by French Literature Publications Company. Reprinted by permission.

INDEX OF

Themes and Ideas